THE 2022 ONE PAGE POETRY *Anthology*

ONE PAGE POETRY

One Page Poetry/The 2022 One Page Poetry Anthology
www.onepagepoetry.com
Printed in the United States of America

The 2022 One Page Poetry Anthology/ One Page Poetry -- 1st ed.

ISBN 9798363981302 Print Edition

All proceeds from the sale of this book will go to the Wildlife Fund and Oceana, two organizations dedicated to the protection of endangered species and the preservation of their natural habitats.

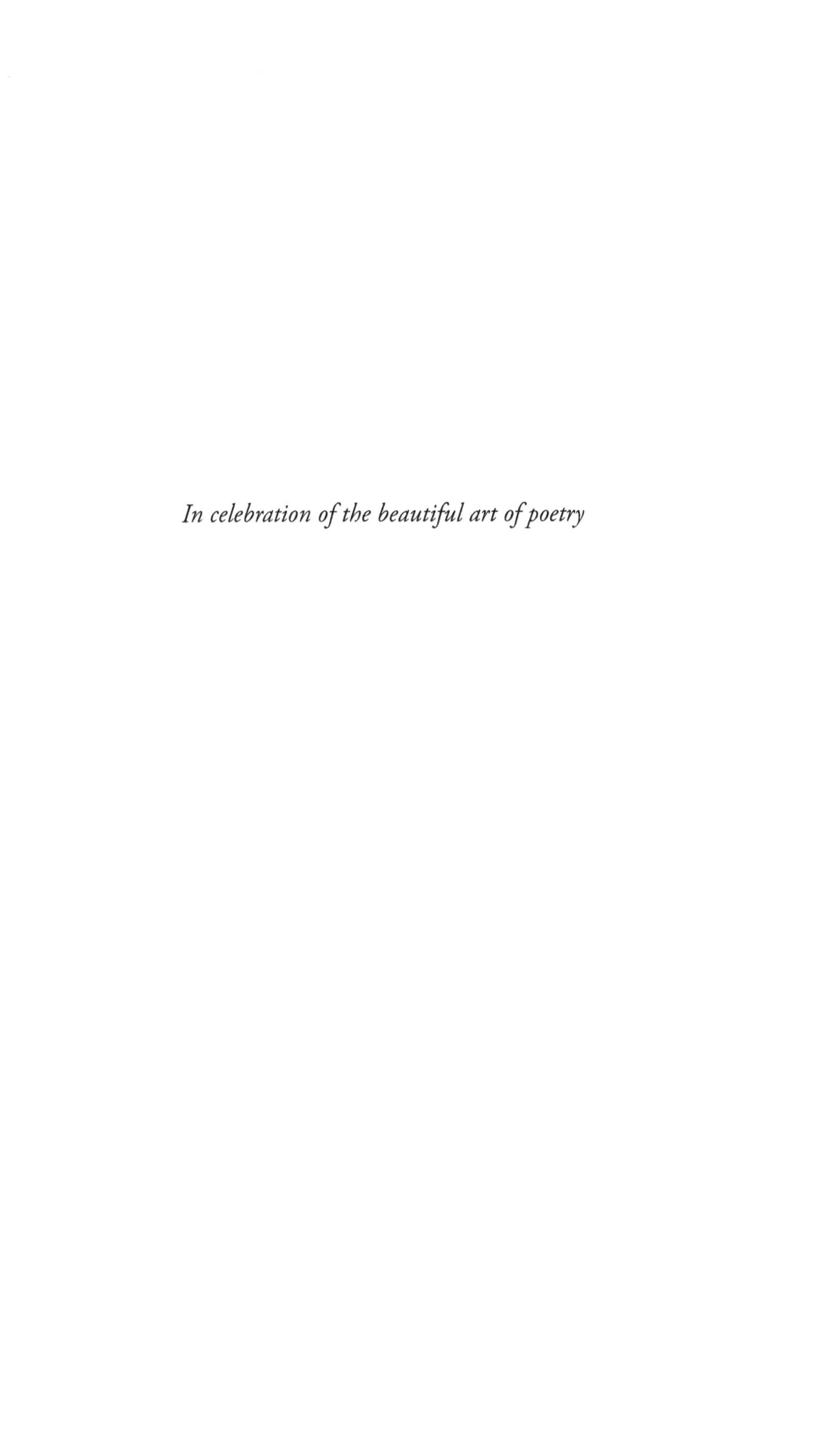

In celebration of the beautiful art of poetry

Publisher's Note

Out of respect for the amazing poets who have contributed to this anthology, the individual poems have not been edited in any way and fully represent the original presentation of each poet. In some cases, poems required formatting to fit the size restrictions of the book and the ebook, but in no way did this formatting change the original wording or grammatical presentation. Since the individual poets represented in this anthology continue to own the copyright to their poems, the poems are not exclusive to this publication, and we encourage the poets to distribute their work as widely as they choose.

Raining Red by Mridvi Khetan

I grew up believing that the rain is red.

Red like the scars mapped across my body,
gifted by a man who colour red embodied
Hot stew for all meals resembled the red sandstone,
which brother went to mine from blood-marked zones
Every day we took a bath in red water,
sourced from a brick well
Everywhere we were blocked by red tape,
sourced from bureaucratic cells

You see, red is omnipresent
It's the colour of resistance but also the colour of our blood
Does this mean we're born to resist?
I resisted red
but how can you, if all you see are corpses - dead.
A memory surfaces in my head,
how my sister was shamed monthly for her red

I can smell it too, you know
The red, a scent of my morning breath
Remnants of the wars fought by words I can only dare to speak in stealth
If red is the paint I've been coloured in, body and bone
It's only logical to see my surroundings in the same tone
So when it rained the other day
I said,
"Ma, see it's raining red today!"

In The Tide by Emily Balchunas

He dragged himself out of bed
       as the sun began to rise.
The seagulls were his alarm,
       he rubbed the dreams from his eyes.
This lighthouse has seen some storms,
       she sways in the night.
The wind whistles through her creaks,
       but never seems to get inside.
Coffee soaked the air,
       the windows let in the sunshine.
The ocean brings a breeze that shifts the house
       from time to time.

The lighthouse was clean and knew his routine,
       this presence of a man.
Her eggshell walls shined a bit brighter,
       her lamp had a certain glisten.
She even seemed to stand a bit taller
       as he occupied her land,
& with every rope he knotted
       the wind would lift his hand.

The keeper of this structure was patient,
       and he cared.
In the morning he'd sing to her
       & at night he'd climb her stairs.
Clicking on her burning light

like brushing back her hair.
With a hot cup of tea
        she thought they both would share.

Fall came and went,
        every winter, time would freeze.
Every night he'd shine her light
        for any ships lost at sea.
As the days would pass them by,
        their nights together began to cease.
No matter how tall she stood,
        she couldn't bring him peace.

One day, the morning breeze came in
        & the sun began to rise.
There were no coffee smells,
        or sleepy groggy eyes.
Gone without a trace,
        like he was taken in the night.
The lighthouse stood empty and still,
        with his memory held inside.

Dare I to say to this very day
        as the sun is sure to rise,
her eggshell halls and walls will wait
        to dance with him again in the tide.

Do You Remember? by Robert Watt

Do you remember the Christmas ball?
Your hair worn up above its wispy strands
And swinging jewels that kissed the neck
Cool and scented with the musk of foreign lands
You rose from a dress the colour of your lips
Plunged a neckline that drew the hungry eye
Onto the eggshell curves and the teasing split
long though never quite revealed the thigh

Do you remember Trafalgar square?
Rushing to the front, running with the madding crowd,
High on passions that quickly gave to laughs or tears,
A rebel stance and voice exuberant and loud
You were strong and lithe, danced into the night,
Filled with beans for a life come recently mature.
We lit candles at both ends and did it all,
Having time and energy to spare for more.

Do you remember Fridays after work
and weekend afternoons lost in sin?
We'd toss our clothes, fall carefree in a fumbling yearn,
Hands buried in hair and greedy for a touch of skin.
We did it all together, hardly left a day apart,
With nothing but ourselves for warmth but happily,
Scraping pennies for bills and budget meals,
Slowly making house then family.

Do you remember how we got so old?
Our faces fell and hair tuned thin and grey.
Focus shifted nearer, the youthful fires cooled,
While the world unnoticed moved away.
We slowed, quietened by relentless years,
Congealed into the people we portrayed;
Staid companions, content with holding hands
Creaking and groaning into life's denoting fade

28 Millimeter Lens by Jessica Zhang

The night is so quiet and violent, yet I'm still listening for sound.
New England August, its crickets. American tires on tired gravel.

These gardens were dying before you arrived.
You watered the flowers and leaves, the spine

of a magnolia tree. The kitchen is empty. In shadows
I still see your figure on the wall; your handprints, their

beautiful symmetry. Yet the morning still comes with its battering ram.
I am familiar with it, with you. Goodbyes; a sound to drown in. These years

have passed so quickly.
The terraces and synagogues disappear from view. Yesterday
I was at the Jewish Quarter in Kraków. I remember the smooth tiles of
the plaza, as clear

as water. The shopkeepers spun guns from chocolate,
birds from almonds and
every taste was sweet. Our palms were cupped to the spring, so drunk

on the idea of us and we, students as careless as doves. You stood there
with your books, your poetry. A voice so soft and unforgiving.

I remember its sound, the cadence;
the horizon flattening

and falling away.

A Glimpse by Jean Stadtfeld

I walked along the creek today
The same creek that several miles downstream
We splashed and laid on rocks on our honeymoon
I saw you today in those dark shaded pools
Darting on their cool, still, watery depths.
I heard you in the echoing
Bubbling of the water over the rocks.
" You walk like a goddess".
I felt a shade of that magical presence
The two of us in love.
A shimmering, glancing vision
It passed over me
And out of time I fell
going with it
Catching a glimpse of its dashing
Fleeting shadow
Just leaving
  good-bye
     good-bye

Sorrows Patchwork by Carly Arave

She has wrinkled the cry.
The letter I licked shut.
She has opened it
to fold and unfold
and refold again.
To let it find the table
every so often
and, more often,
the floor.
The waste.

Read it, she says,
raising it from the bin.
Read it.
Read it again.

I lick the letter shut
and ignore the knock
of the mailbox.
Do you have anything?
it asks.
For me?

When daylight falls,
the thing is curled
under the covers,
asleep.

Read it, she says.
It was made to be read.

And when I won't,
she wrinkles it.
Folds and unfolds.
When I won't.
No one else is going to,
she says.
But someone should.
Someone should.

Read it.
Or, at least,
make it feel
like it has been.

Lonely by Chioma Obi

Lonely is a fear
It's the fear that I wont ever find my person
It's the acceptance that I may always be alone
And trying to be okay with that
But not just alone because no ones around
But alone because no one will see me
It's the fear that if people really see me they will leave
Lonely is the practice of facade
It's the skill of fake laughs and wide smiles
It's the neglectance to my truth and the acceptance of everyone else's
Lonely is the dissatisfaction with who I am
And with being with me
Lonely is the far look into the future thinking I actually might not find it
I actually may never experience what they have
Lonely is the longing for connection so deep it pierces your soul
Lonely is the feeling in your stomach
Lonely is looking at the person beside you and seeing their perfected facade
Or looking at the person to your right and seeing their wide smile
Lonely is seeing your friend mask their sadness with humor
Lonely is knowing the person to your left really isn't okay
Lonely is knowing the person behind you also feels insecure
Lonely is knowing the person in front of you is trying to love
themselves too
Lonely is knowing the person above you is making an effort to stay happy
Lonely is knowing the person beneath you is about to give up
Lonely is knowing that everyone around you is damaged striving to do better
Lonely is knowing everyone has been hurt before

Lonely is knowing that no one person is better than the other
Lonely is knowing that we all think perfection will make us lovable
Lonely is knowing that we were not created to be perfect
Lonely is knowing that everyone is trying
That I try my best too
And now when I look around
I suddenly don't feel that lonely

Downfall by Andrew Graves

Devastation reigns, an ellipses of darkness as impermeable as the night sky.
I dont know where I am, the boy I once was no longer takes hold.
A prisoner of my pain, is all I find myself to be.

Though cuffed and struck down, the boy does remain.
Searching for a light in the thunderous rain.
A means of escape, does not seem likely.

What do I do now, for I had layed down my life.
A total submersion in immeasurable strife.
Yet you were my saboteur.

Perhaps it was a self fulfilling prophecy, paranoia is a friend held near.
A contradiction to the values I hold dear.
Only I was not prepared.

I made a mistake, I gave you my trust.
Something I shall find hard to do again.
But I can try.

A beg, a plea for commiseration by the one who hurt you most.
An ignoramus, you find yourself the host.
I am not okay.

A prisoner of my pain, is all I find myself to be.

I long for freedom, a release from this hell.

It will not strike me down, I wont let the saboteur win.

I will achieve the liberation I seek.

I may not find it today, nor tomorrow.

But I will.

Genesis by Chloe Wang

The missed skip of a heartbeat floats the boundary one-sided death
    another birth of a newborn wound on the chest where red death
seeps from effeminate blooms from beneath a child making room
    for the ghost of youth coiled around His finger. One plighted death
once before resurfacing earth and its mother, promised for a dollar
    and a half to live by it. Years ago I had entered the world abided, death-
bed already pitless under my soles — a perpetual falling, time a line so
    blue tomorrow and yesterday would differ barely. And there was death
on her mind, silken pillow salt drying in the wash, there is death
    in which she is the poem and I am the one who writes.

Empathic by Paul Kindlon

"Hickory Dickory Dock…the mouse. (sniff) That *stupid* mouse!."

Tears welled up in his eyes and became attached to his long eye lashes

They dropped. One by one, onto his clean white shirt.

"Mister Quigley?", little Marsha said, hesitantly, worried, afraid.

"He ran up…the mouse ran up…"

"It's okay Mister Quigley!" Marsha said, consolingly, gently.

She's a kind little girl. And she knows that Mister Quigley is too.

Juxtaposition Physics by Sam George

On the Juxtaposition of Physics and Poetry

When I think about them side-by-side,

I wonder in which do I take more pride.

When I think about my avocation

and how it has become my obsession,

such is the situation in this exposition.

How can I explain this affinity toward poetry?

I'd like to spend my time writing clever rhymes.

I do daily devote to my drafts in order to hone my craft;

in this preparation do I get my satisfaction.

A skill instilled in a youth, rhythmic expressions revealing truths,

both creative and methodical in style, such is my poetic profile.

I write rhymes not only for pleasure, but to partake in lyrical adventures.

However, I do enjoy my career as an engineer.

I like working with engaging minds on complex designs.

I delight in analysis and in unique problem solving techniques.

I have a vast experience in systems development; in essence,

I do enjoy my current profession with great imagination.

However, don't consider me rude, now I'd rather work in solitude.

I prefer writing lyrical compositions to doing scientific experimentation.

I'd rather study the mystery that is poetry:

into its multi-faceted dimensions, I explore the core

of its qualities to compose my many stories

in order to share my contemplations and interpretations

forming into a unifying vision that is my writing.

Of Physics or of Poetry— here's my confession:

I'd rather choose a poet as my profession.

Ode to Blurry Stranger by Christopher Fiander

Ode to Courageous Blurry Stranger

I saw you on that ledge before you lept,
You said you were sad I guess,
Was hard to make out, eight stories down
Could certainly see your cigarette
Whose origin came from who knows when,

Courageous most of all

Pushing off you kept your eyes closed
And I was jealous of your dedication,
To an ID that led you to this weightlessness,
Until you become unbearably heavy.

I've been dreaming.
In the day time
That I could be be a hero to some people
But that will never happen, so

Maybe lend me your bravery
I saw it growing and fading
Between your ragefulyelling, jumping
And your awkward falling, tensing

Ouroboros by Mavis Chan

Static in darkness.
Mist of blue.
Melting into the walls, solitude.

Gift of innocence, stolen.
Serrated teeth,
Devouring myself alive.

Mindless soul,
Staggering on the path of time,
In search of misprinted lies —

O Joy
Floundering about the shores,
Foam to dune, glitters of the sea

Like a setting sun,
Shines their emptiness down my misty-eyes
As I sang the blues.

Pollution by Cassie Lipton

She inhales the second hand smoke.
She likes the way it makes her feel polluted
and a little bit holy.
She holds a lighter three feet in front of his head
and the perspective makes him seem eclipsed
by fire, and it occurs to her
that the scars of other men burn
like galaxies on her skin.
She is cracked like lava fissures in a volcano.
She says, "I am young. I am reckless.
I am neither of those things quite enough."
She could burn so much brighter
Than the ember fading in the ash tray.
Instead, she takes a drag of his cigarette
and it is like she feels him in her lungs.

Racsims by Mohammad Sarvari

Now you get it
Racism!
I don't need to say more
All your minds filling up
with gore
Slavery, name calling, human degrading
If you didn't get it from the beginning,
now its awakening
You know how it started any educated person does.
But why still do it?
Cause it's fun, funny, hilarious?
it's disgusting!
This is the modern generation we should be constructing
A new foundation rising from the old segregation
You might think it's not happening, but it's happening in your life span
Adam Goodes being called a VICIOUS man
When all he was doing was his celebration dance
He was once loved, by all his fans
Until he called out Racism!
Now he's getting slammed!
With all this hatred.
You can only understand if you relate it.
Listen to me! Don't escape it!
Why can't we all get along!
Why can't we all understand this is wrong?

With Muslims it was 9/11, Being white was an obsession, indigenous
people for their impression!

Take notes now! it's a lesson
For all those people who question, I'm saying this so that Racism isn't
deafened
Stop this behaviour now.
You'll be stopping pain.
But if you that if you keep this up,
people won't be, the same.

Adam Goodes being called an APE while in AFL game, he immediately
stopped playing as he was, inflame. As anyone should, I would be too if
i was being called names. And you know what he said later on, "It's not
her to blame." It's her parents who should be ashamed. Be the change
don't be the same.

Muslims get blamed for a group of people who invaded a plane. Give
us a reason why? please explain. Knowing that people can't contain their
anger within their brain so they complain by raising and pointing a finger
at Muslims to release their pain when there's nothing positive to gain!
By ONLY blaming Muslims makes you.

INHUMANE!

Now I'll make everyone understand, universally. If you wanted to be
educated right you go to a university but if you keep this behaviour up
you're going to end up creating a disgusting, diversity.

RACISM!
Now you get it!

The Elegance of Peace by Amber Thompson

Peace, a word that has no direct meaning,
A word so quiet the guns stop shooting,
The school bells stop ringing,
And the cars stop driving.

Peace, a place so quiet,
The trees begin to speak,
Through the bristles in the stump,
Covered by the mossy old grump.
Peace, an indistinct energy,
Afterall, the deer remain eating,
As the children are watching
Near where the bees are talking.

Peace, a feeling so warm and cozy,
The sun feeds the plantations all of her light,
Disintegrating the whites in the clouds,
Causing the rain to fall into crowds

Peace, found deep in the mind,
So deep the noises stop sounding
And the world stops spinning,
But here I am holding peace as it shines.

The Marauding Wolf by S.F. Taha

Flash floods wrecked New York City,
What are the odds for Kuala Lumpur city?
Forest Fire blazed California's National Park
What are the odds for our National Park?
Sea water forever inundating Venice Island
What are the odds for our Penang Island?

Believe you me….
It is no more a cry wolf
It is now a marauding wolf
It is coming after you

One two buckle my shoe,
Three four shut the door,
Five six please mitigate,
Seven eight, lay the adaptation straight,
Nine, ten, No time to begin again,
No more a big fat hen,
Our Earth blue dot no more a zen…

The Morning Wind by Mariah Reynolds

The morning wind
cleared an old cottonwood tree.
The vineyard looks fresh
less wild, more landscaped.
I think I'll be lonely without
it's natural oasis of shade,
it's poetic branches against the sky,
even it's infantry of wasps.
Maybe a memorial should be held.
The insects, field animals, and birds
can gather to tell their stories.
I on the other hand,
will have to go in search
of a new place
to write my letters
in this time of war.

The Storm by Amanda Cockreham

What is it about the storm that calls to me?
The in visionary eye, the dove of the colossal,
Once, when I was little
I danced to the mirror skirt of
 The midnight summer rain
Today, I feed blue jays from my porch
Remembering what it was like to live.

When we were wild
We worshiped the sun, the solstice,
Memories of what it's like to die
We were the apothecary, ate to distinguish
Our land between poison and pleasure

Once when we were wild –
True art was in the sky, rocked us in the ark,
Buried us in the sand, birthed our children, courted our wives
We were the nature
And earth was our man

Today, I am told to pull out shrubs
Today, my lips were sealed shut so that ivy could
Not grow from it, today
I closed my eyes so this vessel's only opening was closed.
Have been silenced for too long –
      Storms brew, ache, foster power
     Not so long ago
          We licked the flame

Toxin by Rhythm Vij

Baby let me tell you something
Don't catch those others spitting names in your mouth
Fight for the chance to lay out your pride
That's the nuance;

Protect your pride as I do
Don't spill what you don't have
What nuance I ask

Baby let me help you
They don't protect you as I do
The nuance is there;

I save my face from the spit
Absorb its moisture on the back of my hand
Protection is what I need
Is that the misconception

Baby please listen
It only hurts you to go there
Why can't you stay;

Im calling them back
They will keep me safe
I see the nuance!

Wonder by Sarah Reinhart

"I think of you every day," he said.

"Then you must be dissatisfied," she replied.

Wonder knew that she was changed.

Her boundaries were amorphous like mercury sliding,

shaping, slipping into the crevices he had made.

Her vision was now limited to the shadow of the certain against the

silhouette of the unknown.

Prismatic shades of variance had blossomed, throwing a riot of colors

against the doors of her cage.

So they walked,

hand-in-hand,

as best they could.

Virginity by Mathilde Reinders

I couldn't walk when he took me home from the party
A pelican I was, holding vomit cautiously in my throat
Next, I remember being under his sheets
His skin melted into mine like hot wax
His last drink tasted sweet when he threw his tongue down my throat
like an eager fisherman
throwing a line.
He climbed down my torso to a place he seemed to know better than myself
He was hungry
Inhaled me like a dog at dinner
Excitement and pain danced on my skin
He came back up to meet my eyes and rolled on some plastic he prom-
ised would protect me
I lay there
One minute feeling like an hour but a night feeling like a blink
He entered me
Not with a knock but with a key
How does he have a key?
I must have given him one
Or maybe the door was already open?
"Its ok" I tell myself
Eyelids comforted my pain
"It will be over soon"
My moans of pain misheard as pleasure

It finished
His touch formed a blanket around me
Comfort
He molded himself to fit my piece of the jigsaw
Squeezed insecurity from me like puss from a wound
Until I felt loved
He rubbed my back and stroked my legs
A piece of trash and a queen simultaneously I felt
The next day I left his house as I entered it
Unable to walk, but happy i'd grown up

Wonderland by Alexandra Cabral

One foot over the edge,
then neither.
I have been seduced by the rabbit hole again.

I am not troubled by this.
I like it here, it's comfortable.
Predictably unpredictable

I tell myself; no - convince myself,
I am not falling,
but floating.

A beautiful illusion.

Though my moments with euphoria are slowly depleting,
while my moment of impact ensues.
I pretend not to know.

I still hold onto you,
and hoard the consolation you provide.
Until my collision with reality.

Shards of me scattered.
I will pick up the pieces,
though I will not get them all.

I am not troubled by this,
for I have decided
to end this war of freedom from myself.

I do fear though,
my dear Mad Hatter,

as Alice always returns to wonderland.

The Dream by Raquel Hertzler

Slip on through, you appear in my unconscious.

Frustration over comes my existence.

Disappear into my dimension that's where you exist in my

Imagination.

All That They Said by Saye Kamal

"Breathe! Breathe! breathe!" they said
Though she had no lungs

"Listen! Listen! Listen!" they said
Though she had no ears

"Look! Look! Look!" they said
Though she had no eyes

"Cry! Cry! Cry!" they said
Though she had no tears

"Scream! Scream! Scream!" they said
Though she had no fear

"Sing! Sing! Sing!" they said
Though she had no voice

"Dance! Dance! Dance!" they said
Though she had no legs

"Die! Die! Die!" they said
Though she had never lived

Another Poem by Gabriel Boykin

A Christian
Here I sit to write again.
Nothing more but me, my God, and my pen.
Should I use this blessed moment to confess a history of sin,
Or instead contemplate the riches of life with Christ in heaven?

Oh, the wondrous blessing an empty page is!
Upon which the possibilities are endless!
Picture this:
A writer, senseless, sets himself down before God and repents,
Then pens something like this:
"Look to the true King with utter reverence"
Our bodies are living sacrifices, giving off heaven-ward holy incense,
Do you get this?

The pen is mightier than the sword,
Young men may disagree, but behold,
Men with pens tend to die old;
Unless, indeed, they write something that truly matters,
In which case all forces of hell sets its sight to shatter
The blessed writing of a wretched man,
Who was blessed to meet the great I AM.

It's been said dying is easy, living is harder.
Indeed, it has a tinge of truth, but I would barter:
It is in our nature to do what it takes to be a survivor.
I'd say to live for something you wouldn't die for is hardest.
Say what you will, I know that you will, but regardless,

If you won't die for Christ, you won't live for Christ!
To be born again you must die, I call that insight!
He didn't just die for us to live, alright.
He died that we might die;
He rose that we might also rise.

We be dead men, in Him we are given new life,
And He, brethren, is worth whatever the sacrifice.

Cecilia by Wil Monisera

(Cecilia: Derived from the Latin word caecus meaning "blind")

Watch your step and I will hold your hand as you go

Your face was my recurrent dream, even before we said "Hello"

Watch out for the wind, it knocks one over as it blow

Can I call you "astonishing"? Is that even apropos?

If I had only one request upon a majestically rapid star

It would be for seeing eyes and a mirror.

For you to know how breathtaking you are

You have never gazed upon the moon shining over peaceful water

Lean yourself on me, not a chance you will ever totter

But as we travel, I realize… it is I that needs you to remain upright

Numerous secrets must fall upon the ears of the night

A walk without you, is one where I would tumble

This is reality. Do not count me humble

Cecilia, lean on me. As much as I lean on you

You see clearly, without any physical view

An ardent sun and torrid glee

All from someone who cannot see

A bright girl, knowing life as a dream

Most definitely the better half of our team

It freezes me in place…your smile in the sun

Any cause for gray and dull become undone

Those eyes…somehow they are staring back

Supplying all of the eluding strength I lack

Tears and frowns are strangers to your mind

Maybe you should lead the way, and I will walk behind

Cecilia, in word it is preposterous at its core

But a sightless dove showed me the door

Regardless of what the doctor said, we know the truth

A power exists within you. It turns the withering into youth

So, go on and walk gracefully on your route

I will follow closely. Life's conquest is absolute

A Pretty Little Morsel by Nathaniel Boyd

"You're a pretty little morsel" – said the man in the coon-skinned hat.
As he walked toward my daughter, his pistol just like that.

And as I fingered my rifle, my good eye on his heart,
I knew I'd give 'em what was comin' to 'em if they stepped in the dark.

Two pairs of boots entered the foyer, sendin' her shriekin' down the hall,
Right into the black, black corridor, where I's waitin' for y'all.

With two booms that shook the earth, the wind faded away.
'Cause Old Man Jefferson wasn't havin' it today.

Dress By Charlotte Cundiff

I am so pretty when she puts me on
On bright summer days,
She wears me out like her favorite song

From a pile of clothes
I'm the one that she chose
Spinning around her sister's room
Enveloped in scarlet,
A flower in bloom

Rosebuds and green leaves
I fit like a daydream
She zips me up for the first date
When he sees her, his eyes gleam
Stands up to greet me
He walks her home and they kiss at the gate

Over the years I lay alone
Collecting dust in her aging home
Over time I've come to find
I'm simply a memory in the back of her mind
Late nights spent on the phone
Family dinners and "How much you've grown!"
Pretty friends and petty crimes
Please put me on again, just one last time.

A Vampire in Versailles by August James

It wasn't in some dark alley, or the late-night walk through the park,
not like in the movies.
Something much more cinematic, or dramatic, I could never remember which.

It was the class trip, visiting the palace of Versailles.
It began well enough, all splendor and awe,
much like the other monuments and castles we had visited.

I, being rebellious, or stubborn, I can never remember which,
decided to sneak down a corridor labeled, zone réglementée.

A right and a left, lead me to a polished marble door,
inlaid with intricate gold patterns, and swirls of silver.
The handle had been replaced by a lion's head made of onyx.

I pushed the heavy door open, revealing a dimly lit extravagance.
Silk and stately frames decorated high walls.
In the center was a large four-poster bed.
Atop of which sat Maria Antoinette.

In her lap was a lifeless brunette, mouth open, a silent scream,
Maria's teeth still sunk deep into her neck.

Blood spilling like ruby rivulets down her breast,
onto a brilliant white satin sheet.
A few misbehaving drops splattered the floor just beneath her head.

She looked up slowing, with hunted cerulean eyes…that was long ago
now…Je meurs de faim.

Hardcover Heart by Desiree Graf

i open up
my hardcover heart
it bleeds
don't break the spine
you put your index
on taciturn pages
and read
between the lines

Mebin and Cervus by Daniel Molina

Journey on myriapod legs, quick Mebin!
Your innards, a vacuous wasteland. Now,
Thousand steps by myriad feet are slow—
Prey finds refuge in its lair, its haven.
His temples with exertion are laden
WIth the heft of a much-maligned, bronze sow,
And drenched anew via murder by crow.
Seven years of hard toil, uncle Laban!

Sheer stone turns as rich as soil! Elusive
Cervus, whose splintered bones have failed you,
And prostrate on the low bluff, obtrusive
Are the overlong shanks that shadowed you.
Famined mauvins now revel, allusive
To a bite of meat, rosemary, and yew.

Dried Out by Lee J

Grass left alone grows tall yet brittle.
Bending to the whims of the wind.
Each blade sharp.
Grows higher and higher.
Taller and taller.
Dryer and dryer.
Not a single drop of moisture.

Grass, however, keeps growing.
Not caring how stale it has become.
Not caring how parched.
It still grows higher and higher.
Taller and taller.
Dryer and dried out.
Finally dried out.

I Am a Snake by Sydney Doty

February 5th, 2022. 3 months and 3 weeks sober.

I'm shedding my skin. The universe had to make me uncomfortable so I would move. So I would be willing to change.

When a snake first sheds its skin, it undergoes extreme discomfort. Its skin is itchy. It hides from the sun, because its brightness is too harsh.

But it does not fight it.

It has outgrown its previous covering. it no longer serves it. When the old skin chips away, the new skin is sensitive. Raw.

But, over time, it strengthens. The snake can go out in the sun and receive its warmth once again. Previous relationships and situations no longer served me. That constant unease, discomfort, that constant itch, was the universe telling me," move, change, before they move you."

Predation by Rana Kurt

One step forward
Or two steps back?
What will become of the clownfish with pride?
What will become of the momentary shame?
I realize with my tail between my legs
That I no longer want
This instability of prowess
Of inexperience
Of beauty
We judge the lion that shreds any piece of inferiority in its way
And we judge the tuskless narwhal
Who has potential and how should they use it?

On Moving Forward by Rem Martin

The gentle patter of small feet
Draws my attention from the blistering heat
A young girl stands off in the distance
Shrouded in a ghostly aura that contends her existence

Long matted hair, a sickening crown
Only serves to compliment her prominent frown
Bloodshot eyes bore into my soul
Searching for the secrets I might have stole

I know this child, her frail sunken face
Will forever haunt my heart's hallowed space
For we are eternally one and the same
Separated only be time and name

I long to wrap her in my arms
Swear to keep her sheltered from harm
Our old scars may be rubies on our skin
But now they simply show where we have been

"Come now young child
Your fate is not sealed
There is still a whole world to be healed
Let us be the light and helping hand
We once thought only existed in Neverland

Take my hand and we can soar
To a play where your past haunts you no more
There is nothing more I need from you
Just laugh and play like children do"
For one so young to rage and fight
I'm honestly surprised she has kept her light
But now her soul can lay to rest
Knowing that she did her very best

"I'll take up the mantle my dear
Be free of worry, I am here."

Saturday Matinee - An Ode to Cyrano by Noelle Gallagher

My soul has dusted off its weighty yoke
and for a moment, sat with the divine,
And though it shimmered just beyond my reach
it called – an urgent cry that I might find
A glimmer of all truth if I could stop
a while, and stopping, let the moment breathe,
And in that moment time would cease its haunt
and grant to me a much needed reprieve
From daily woes that wrap around my lungs,
Obscuring all belief that I'm alive,
But now I see beyond that shrouded veil
That I have done no more than just survive.
How strange that make-believe could quell that fear,
That acting seems to me an honest truth,
That scripted words do more than entertain –
They gift to me undeniable proof
Of purpose, perhaps to be and to know
That my small heart was made for something more.
These dogged days on earth ascend the daily grind,
If only hearts like ours dare to explore
Beyond the reaches of our boundless web
Of lies that fill the seconds, minutes, years,
That bleed into our deepest depths of self
By preying on our fundamental fears.
Yet through another ruse we see the world
Not as it is, but as it might yet be.
In that safe space our walls are broken down,
Confronted with our own humanity.

The peace I found is sure to fade away
As life speeds on much as it did before,
But in this moment I've transcended self
And found for my now restless heart a cure.
Within my brain I'll keep the secret safe
That life is more than wake, work, eat, and die.
I'll tap into that feeling I have found
So that my soul need not forget to fly.

See me? Hear me? by Ray Anthony Cadiz

Much like the Hermit Thrush,
out of sight and full of song.
One trill in the grand mutation;
a choir of melodic chirrupy;
yet, fearful of its sweet but melancholic solo ballad,
imperfect vibrato and unique melody;
composed of quavering minor notes and trembling sharp tones.
From a summit mount, or the forest crown
melodious and harmonious fervidly bound.
Scaling life's inequities, I am.
See me; Hear me.

A Dying Star by Olivia Tang

Paint a story
Across the sky
The story of a star
And his silent cry

An ember in the wind
Fading into the darkness
How could the universe
Be so heartless

How lonely it must be
To wane into history
What's to come next
being a mystery

Farewell he said
And he looked to the sky
"I simply hope to not
Be forgotten in time"

Spice To My Dish by Zachary Fox

Be that it may, the secret ingredient is 'dread':
A familiar set of letters on an inked page, passing by in turn of a
cookbook-
Vital, this taste of silence, what overwhelms the meal.
This dish cannot maintain its own potent stink,
And it draws a vile color.
Though reluctant,
The integrity of my dish is consistent.
It is safe.

Withdrawn-
Hesitant-
Uncertainty-
'Dread'.
The silence becomes palpable; my compliments to the chef–

–though I find myself sick.

Unfortunate and desperate as I may be-
The brew becomes less complex.
A pinch of 'dread'-
And there is ease.

But- I am still miserable
as this taste careens my throat.
I- do not understand?
To name the dish a 'Shrinking Violet'
Though I blossom as a wallflower,

'Dread' remains all the same.
My own speech, I cannot trust, lacking this articulation-
The remainder towards this silence becomes refuge,
Comforted in my own craft, guaranteed by the illusion of eloquence.
Doubt is strong, once words are spoken over this dish.
The dish is perfect, but it is spoiled.
Not without 'dread'.

I am sickly, but I am safe-
Turmoil in my pyramid.
Necessities lost but numbness maintained.
Try not to think- taste.
When indulging this dish,
You'll only vomit.

And you won't remember having cooked it red.

The Girl Who Stares Out the Window by Elise Horn

In a neighborhood lies a house there
In the house, lies a girl who likes to stare

She stares out the window
With purpose and plea
Her eyes look for something
Like identity

She looks at passing people
To find what's inside
She can only be seeing
The pure child that hides

She sees something odd
But can't figure it out
She sees some facade
Something to think about

She questions her identity
As fall rolls around
She questions her mortality
As the leaves turn brown

Comes the winter
Hither and thither
Struggles to find herself
And starts to whither

Years pass on
She turns to dust
The house she once lived in
Turned to rust

Some pass by
And still, see
A broken window
With two eyes of plea

Eyes of blue
And eyes of mad
Eyes of clue
And eyes of sad

They look again
And question their sight
A sense of fear they feel
And something not right

The eyes have disappeared
That was once there before
The eyes that they feared
Will haunt them once more

The Lucky Ones by Elizabeth Buhr

Canceled plans and long hospital stays,
An early baby is on the way.
Magnesium and steroid shots,
Just try to - make - labor - stop.

Plan A, plan B, plans C through F,
There are no more backup plans left.
Baby must come now, it can not wait,
Or there could be a deadly fate.

Baby arrives, a team swoops in,
No time for any skin to skin.
Does dad follow the baby or stay with mom?
Why does either feel so wrong?

Mom is wheeled by baby's bed,
Then to a room elsewhere she is led.
She misses the first diaper and feeding the next day,
But her body isn't yet okay.

Discharge day is hardest by far,
Tears stream down while in the car.
The most unnatural a mom will feel,
Leaving the hospital makes it real.

Future days are spent in an old NICU chair,
Some filled with hope and others despair.
Endless washing causes hands to crack,

Bringing bottles of pumped milk in a pack.
The monitors, the beeping, the screaming alarms,
Chaos surrounds the baby in her arms.
Baby breathes and baby grows,
Baby will go home at some point they know.

In a place full of early arrivals,
She's grateful for the chance at survival.

Her family is one of the lucky ones.

The New Christmas Leader by Valentina Santillana

It was that time of the season, the cold and the snow.
The Christmas lights blinking with their colorful glow.

We were all at the corner of the neighborhood park,
The puppies excited to be out after dark.

I was the leader in my part of town,
"Remember, no barking, we must keep it down".

The meeting with Santa was ready to start,
The tails were all wagging, excitement at heart.

I gave out instructions to both young and old.
"This is a secret, it must never be told".

"Now keep your eyes open, today is the day.
And he'll come and be gone in his magical way".

When all of a sudden, a "whoosh" sound was heard.
And he landed right there, like a beautiful bird.

His eyes were a twinkle, his voice soft and clear
"Does everyone know the reason they're here?"

The pups were confused, they hadn't a clue,
"We're here for a job" said one of the crew.

"You certainly are" he said with a grin.
"Your job is important, you must let me in".

"Come Christmas Eve you must leave out the key.
So I can come in and place gifts by the tree".

"And remember, no telling, no child must know
That it's actually pups that let me in from the snow".

And with that he was gone, with sparkling eyes,
As we stared and we searched for his sled in the skies.

I looked at my gang, and the message was clear.
"We've all got a job, it's that time of the year!"

This Christmas was special, as leader, my last.
My old legs were tired, they weren't as fast.

I remember the day I was chosen to lead,
They gave me the honors, thanks to my speed.

I'd been watching a puppy, Flash was his name.
He was fast, he was strong, and up to the game.

I called him, "Say Flash, are you ready to shine?"
"You bet" he responded "This Christmas is mine!"

"You must follow my lead and learn all the tricks
Make sure, as the leader, that everything clicks".

"I'm sure I can do this", said Flash, feeling proud.
"It's not always that easy", I muttered aloud.

"There's snow storms and mix-ups and keys we can't find.
But we have to help Santa, no gift left behind."

"And we mustn't ignore, there are homes with no pet,
That also have children, we cannot forget.".

We have to beat Santa with his twinkling eyes
And leave out the keys before he arrives."

"Now Flash, carry the message, the mission is clear
It's your job to make sure we bring Christmas cheer".

Flash got so excited he jumped up and down,
"I'm the new leader!" he barked all over town.

The other pups praised him, "you're the best for the job!"
And they all headed home, as a bustling mob.

And on his first Christmas, Flash did his job well.
I showed him my tricks and he bid me farewell.

I watched from afar as the keys were put out,
All doors would be opened, I hadn't a doubt.

A Friend Cried That Night by Jeremy Knowles

Look at me-
It's time for roadside therapy
Everything is ok, just breathe
Cry it out if need be

A broken heart heals,
making you stronger
Time knows the remedy,
and so does laughter

Regret will flood,
followed by sadness
It'll fade away
with retrospection

Let yourself feel,
and be gentle
Protect your energy
like it's a temple

The Survivors' Star By Eliza Sible

If you look up at the sky, on a certain hour, of a certain night,
you'll see a special star

It's filled with childrens' cries and womens' wooziness,
seen but not said from afar

A liar might tell you it's built from love
But a man will tell you the story of King David, "sent from above"

A story of its birth so beautiful and promising
With an end so horrible and grovelling

It's like a tattoo that always stays
Or a burn imprinted by a farmer's craze

It twinkles a bluish glow
Like the tears an unhappy widow would bestow

When you wish upon this star
Pray for the animals drowned in tar

For they were trapped and died in black
Still watching the life they'll never get back

But forever, it sparkles and gleams
Letting you keep a hold of your dreams

They'll tell you it's all imaginary
You tell them it's only temporary

Look up at the sky
And remember the cry

Of past people like you
And all who are new

It will keep your name in hand
And give it to the dusk's marching band

Who will play in your dreams at night
And make the next day a little more bright

This special star
Seen from afar
Is for survivors
The Survivors' Star

Are You Tired Little One by Jenna Nancarrow

Are you tired, little one?
Tired of the mess that gets the best of you?
Of the criss-cross of empty vesicles,
that blow through city streets, tumbling,
endlessly, towards their target of
indifference?

Are you tired, little one?
Have the old-world parade-makers
and war mongers been mean again,
faceting your life to peer through,
evaluate, and, with a headless shake,
assign a non-value to your pain?

Are they proud, little one?
That they've spent the years of plenitude
in arrogant isolation, for the restitution
to rest on much shorter shoulders,
and the ever-wilting wonders of our
once resplendent Mother
turned to ashes and electrons?

Do they cry, little one?
In voices as loud as we when we call
to curb the coming onslaught of
retribution? It's our future,
bleaker than the depressed, distressed
past from which it was forged.
Lift your head, little one.
Open your eyes.
Soon, they'll all be dead,
and the Earth will be nothing but sky.

A Winter Moment by Preston Sigmon

Despite the gentle hum of distant life
Silence whispered softly in the still December air
Every breath I cycled through my lungs
Refreshed the warmth inside my chest
With a rush of winter
Frost fully formed beneath my feet
Frozen drops of dew glistening in the grass below
Little beads of light
Gleaming bright
Like the stars in the sky above
Neck cocked back
Staring speechless
Through the silhouettes of naked trees
Into the deep expanse
A blanket of night
Wrapping the world inside
The arms of time and space

Becoming Me by Jessica Tinkle

I can't be what you want me to be
I have to be what I'm meant to be
Even if that means you're disappointed in me
Then at least that means you and me can be free

Embroideries by Leonard Johns

I close the hand,
The lifted,
The creased,
The weightless,
The unashamed hands rest with the faithless.

The hand speaks to me,
As it seeks new ground to cut patterns and insignia,
Embroideries unravel to the tunes of their forebearers.

Through my clenched and steady fingers.
Calling me to bind,
Struck are these hands of mine.
Thunder, lightning, and fury,
Have rocked them.

Blessed are the wearers of my heart,
Taken by the colours, fabric, cut.
That which is yours,
Was once mine,
Did you know?

Hidden Away by Maria Paula Murcia Nieto

Is it that my heart is not meant to be held?
Am I to keep it tucked away?
my eyes are glued to watch fortunate hands
find each other in sweet embrace
while my own hands wither in the cold
hiding in the pockets of my coat
and the feeling of my chest aches
why is that I have to wait? to wait to be loved
Am I just the girl walking by?
the one who stares too much at the sky
because looking in front of me is facing reality
and the reality is, I long for a hand to hold
a hand to pull me in and wrap me in warmth
a gentle kiss on my lips to send me in flames
but I'm simply a match that will never be lit
I want an endearing smile, a smile only for me
one that sends me away with the wind
yet im only to be grounded by where I stand
and I just stand as a lonely tree
a tree that's too used to the cold
no longer expecting leaves to grow
Will I slowly wither away as I think,
Is it that I'm not meant to be loved?
am I to keep my heart in its cage?

I Cannot Speak Today by Lukas English

"I cannot speak today"
is what my sister used to say
when telling us about her day
about how, "farming was our great dismay".
"Mistake, I mean, I just misspoke…
misspake, I mean". Oh what a joke!
A grin she drew across our masks,
our brightened faces bursting laughs.
And so, to end the farce with force,
she said, "because I cannot speak. Of course".
On this, her first day of ninth grade,
at that same school in which I'd made
myself. Surrounded by such a wealth
of opportunity, chances made for you'n'me
to figure out just who we'd be.
On that, my last day of high school,
thinking that it would be cool
if I stayed silent, stayed away,
said that "I cannot speak today".
But by some miracle of god,
a hundred pairs of hands applaud,
and I walk up. Me! I'm awed.
Under the lights, in front of all
one hundred souls: my curtain call.
I stumbled over all my lines
of friends helping me through hard times,
friends helping me sign up for band,
friends climbing high, lending a hand.

Well. Really a rope, or a jazz note,
but as I stumbled on I spoke,
my smile helping me to cope
with all one hundred faces,
sitting silent in their places.
And then, I saw, in every pew,
smiles adorning their mouths too!
My joy, my confidence, it grew,
it soared! And though tonight it may have poured,
a violent rain, tonight I live without the pain
of regret. Because those hundred souls I met
with my word, and each and every one, they heard.
And though mistakes I may have made,
a love, my smiling face betrayed,
reciprocated by grade,
all because I spoke that day.

Me and Marc Maron by Lucas Hardwick

Last night I dreamed
me and Marc Maron
were record shopping
in a Quentin Tarantino film.
He said, "Hey, buddy!
You don't have to be a Steely Dan fan,
man."
I said, "Don't worry. I'm not."
And then I scratched my head
and said, "But I do like Scotch whisky."
Marc said, "I don't do that no more,
buddy."
And we left
without our copies
of Hitchcock Blondes.
That's a made-up band,
in a made-up place,
and if I had to guess,
they're probably punk rock,
or jazz.
We'll ask Quentin at the unemployment office,
where we get our unemployment checks,
that pay for unemployment Scotch.
Not the kind Steely Dan drinks.
The kind the Italians drink
in those sleazy Italian films
like Quentin Tarantino makes.

In this turbulent sea we call life
you've been my one constant, my rock.
When the endless waves of pain
engulfing and stifling my soul
try to pry me from your arms,
I want to let go.
But in the silence of the night,
when all is still and fanciful dreams
play like reels behind their eyes,
my piercing scream breaks the silence.
And you're gently shaking me awake
and holding me until
my nightmare dissipates,
and the silence returns
as the night recaptures its still.

My Constant Rock by Laura Popovici

In this turbulent sea we call life
you've been my one constant, my rock.
When the endless waves of pain
engulfing and stifling my soul
try to pry me from your arms,
I want to let go.
But in the silence of the night,
when all is still and fanciful dreams
play like reels behind their eyes,
my piercing scream breaks the silence.
And you're gently shaking me awake
and holding me until
my nightmare dissipates,
and the silence returns
as the night recaptures its still.

Ode to an Enemy by Brianna Mason

It's not that I wasn't expecting it,
I could tell by the way you didn't seem to care.
Conversations were left unfinished.
Acknowledgments were left unaware.

Accountability held me down
Like a rabbit in the face of a hound.
Blood red teeth dug deep in my skull.
Left for dead, left unwhole.

Despite your tactics, I could tell
That deep down you're just like me

You're not the wolf you think you are
Not strong enough to leave a scar.

Above your smile, I see your glare.
Your head is filled with despair.
I can tell you feel regret,
But don't think that I'll forget.

Behind your mask I see you hide.
You fake your smile.
You fake your pride.

One day I hope you see,
That inside you're just like me

Papaver by Hannah Capone

The times of doom
Once passed away
Restore the day to old
The passed who laid
Their souls of gold
the standing bloom, they wore

And so rises the papaver
Red from blood and gore
The mockingbird
Mimics the lore
Of winds that share the word
And so they say, the papaver
Gather 'round the core
Of fields of green
And skies of blue
For they have been there before

Puzzle by Kenneth Kidd

A long time ago when my life first began
I came into the light and drew my first breath
And the first piece of my puzzle was made
As I began my journey from my birth to my death

The years went by from toddler to teen
With pieces added daily as I was molded
Into a unique one-of-a-kind sentient being
Who would morph and mature as my life unfolded

I experienced infatuation and puppy love and then
At seventeen I found her working at an ice cream shop
When my friend and I stopped by for an ice cream sundae
I knew she would be my mate until my heart would stop

But fate would have her leave me to go with another
And that piece of my puzzle was pulled from my board
While my life continued and other pieces were added
As I searched for another who could not be ignored

And one day my puzzle was almost finished
With that one stubborn piece left to place
I tried piece after piece as the years went by
Frustrated with the incomplete life I must face

Then forty-two years from that day we departed
She came back and it seemed we had never split
I wrapped my arms once again around her
As the final piece of my puzzle was a perfect fit

The Books in the Broken Building (Ode to Ukraine) by Bella Wright

Longing
Some say that an object as still as book cannot possibly feel
But all I feel is longing

Longing to be held
Longing to be loved
Longing to be laughed at
cried over and spelled

There is no one left to stroke the binding
And admire our textured titles
They are all gone and hiding
From an evil I've named Vile

So now our tattered pages' vocal cords
Have long grown tired
We sit here on this shelf
and feel like we've been fired

The sun shines through the wall
Blasted off
But its light is cold

Its orange light is like the fire that skipped us in the dark
The fire I wish would come again
Because if my pages feed that fire
I'll have made my final spark

The Soothsaying Pioneer by Joe Falco

Some carry the belief that life is a predetermined journey, and that we are all just passengers on a tour of our own lives. However, one can grace this dogma with rough seas by pursuing an arduous endeavor. During this quest, unwavering grit and patience must be equipped to traverse through the rugged terrain of hardship. While in transit, embrace the wear and tear, display their scars like a badge of honor. Bypass the naysayers and express gratitude towards those who have offered you a lift. If you find yourself at a dead end, regroup and reroute to a different peak. When you have reached the summit of your goal, savor your day in the sun. As dusk approaches, reflect and realize the most beautiful truth; We are at the helm of our fleet. Not an occupant along for the ride, rather, a soothsaying pioneer that envisions their future, but carves their own path. Don't settle on this new conquered ground. Rest, but on the dawn of a new day, aim your compass towards where your heartstrings strum and steadily track down your dreams.

This Old Young Woman by Jacqueline Smith

Wearing decades, this old-young
woman cannot see through milky
eyes. A spirit of glimmering pearl
hatched like a grain of sand but crumbling
inside her frame are days of bone-weary
fatigue that carried man and married
progeny to knowledge of themselves.

She bends now, rages at their appearance,
leaning to catch a breath of youth that
holds the minds' spark steady in the
nothingness of her days; once full of doing.
Still she counsels, consoles and gathers tears
and trials to lay upon her back, bending low;
coming closer to the earth.

The curve she carries questions why
as purpose dwindles. Trickling sand, the
hourglass, to the bottom heaps.
Time like a blanket covers all; shrouded like
goodnight. A morning still to waken will
stretch the moment with the end in sight and
still she might hear their call, whispering one and all.

Memories in Separation by Daniel Ireton

My heart, it bleeds for you. My eyes, they tear for you. I miss you. Yes, I miss you.

Even when you were miles away from me. In those moments of separation, you were there with me. Yes, even now you are still with me.

Every moment of every day I reflected on your beauty. In those moments of reflection, I saw you. Yes, In my imagination I still see you.

My mind, it dwells on all the wonderful moments that we shared. I am thinking about us. Yes, I still think about us.

The love that we made with its expression and its display. It moved my heart for you. Yes, the thought of it still moves my heart for you.

Whenever you pulled me into your arms. I melted in your warm embrace. Yes, I still imagine that warm embrace.

From the scent of your skin, to the smell of your hair. Your essence has never left me. Yes, your essence is still with me.

My heart, it still bleeds for you. My eyes, they still tear for you. I miss you. Yes, I still miss you.

In The Beginning by Yahudiyah Yahudah Yisrael

When the sun made it first peak then, I wake from sleep, as my day goes by, I hear the wind fly and I sigh. I look around and all I see is dirt, and water. I ask myself in a little time what will I be? Then I remember that time is like waterfall it's been flowing since time had begun. A cloud covers the sky. Pitter-patter goes the raindrop, and I'm still a little seed, and in a week who knows what I'll be.

I'm digging through the dirt trying to find my way out, I've grown a little head, I'm still in a seed waiting patiently till it's the right time for me. I reach the surface; I never knew there were so many beautiful things living right above me. There's a bird that's sing, a cricket that chirps, and a grasshopper that leaps, but then I see something weird and different from the others and me. It's a weird creature who has feet, I wonder what they do to help nature. Soon I see one right above me not looking at me but one that is right near me. My, my, what beautiful creatures I've seen, some big, some small, they all are different but are here for the same job.

It's been 2 weeks I've grown from a sprout to a sapling. A sapling's a little big but not big enough. Don't worry I won't give up until I'm fully grown up. It's been a month already, and I'm still growing. How can this be? When will I be a fully grown tree? In a week, a month, or two? I don't know, only time knows. Until then I'll leave my story for time to tell.

38.75 by Kyia Clayton

It cost $38.75 to ship my stepfather's ashes.

I packed them inside a used box with bubble wrap and books and a small blanket we had in the back of the car for the beach, a wash of relief as I walked out of the post office - laced with a pang of guilt.

For three months I have been hiding his ashes in closets, the car, the back patio- no one wanted them around, so I kept moving them to avoid the inevitable complaints. I had to wait until his niece was back at her farm where they will be buried.

They let Catholics be cremated now if their ashes are buried!

I chose not to show them to my mother, even though I had a lovely wooden box made by a local woodworker to put them in - I couldn't take the possible emotion, her memory loss made this easier.

Nursing him through his death was enough. A job I didn't choose but did to perfection-fighting palliative care to keep him at home and having to take on the role of attending to his dying body … my head awash with new grey hairs. A gift from the stress.

He wasn't a horrible man, but my life is so much easier now that he is dead. He was a patriarch, self-focused, demanding, emotionally immature and sometimes verbally cruel.

He had been a Jesuit priest for the first part of his life, pushed in by his mother and seduced out by his first wife, a woman who managed him. Her death a surprise, within two months he was engaged to my mother, this says a lot about them both.

I had feared his death for years- twenty-five to be exact.

Afraid of his lack of future planning for my mother,

terrified of my mother without a husband,

consumed by the what ifs.

Now his ashes are on the way to the mainland.

He liked to take road trips.

A Body of Sleeping Bones by Katrina Lemaire

Jerked from slumber, the sun is high, summoning the first crack of wake.

Pulled into fresh clothing, she sighs, ready to take.

Draped in black and gold, boots clomp down concrete, drawing eyes that are less discreet.

Descending downstairs, swiping a card with a ss-click, the day commences.

Tap, tap, tap, the ends of rubber soles bounce on laminate floors, mimicking the clap-clap-clap of silent internal applause. The first transaction is complete.

-It's an extra fifteen off? Amazing! -Can I return this?
-I have a return."
-Can you price check this?
-I'm here to pick up an order.
-You're name is beautiful.
-I love your necklace.

Sounds fill up space. Entering the canals of a receiving ear, a place of memory. A list.

A place of repetition.

Her ammunition. Firing off the same responses, the same answers.

Her eyes glimpse digital clock numbers, pattering keys on nimble fingers, typing away the enter buttons, waiting to break.

She needs a break.

Rumblings, grumblings, gurglings, inside her stomach curdle, her arms heavy with ligaments and hunger, waiting no longer. Time has ticked to three in the noon. Not a moment too soon. Clothing whooshes on air, barely clinging to the limbs hanging by muscle and tissue, swaying back and forth, the knee rises and descends down stone stairs, pop-crack, pop-crack, at the breaths exhaled inside marrow. There is sorrow.

Deep, nestled in the hairs of a mind picked clean of energy, three more hours await. Tick. Tick. Click. A smile spread on her face like warm butter on toast. She has done the most, a customer smiles back, a break, a crack in the day. Hope. She has hope. Tick. Tick. Click. Done. She has done. Dragged to a home of solace, the limbs recline, no longer in decline. The breaths ease, the mind purged of voices, of sounds, of lists, of names. The arms hang, the fingers twitch, the feet repose, the air pulled softly into lungs.

Asleep. High above in her thrones, she is a body of sleeping bones.

A Murmur of Memory by Audrey He

I rise at dawn.

The Caribbean greets my window sill,
gentle, quiet.

Before the sun rises, the air is cool,
providing
a momentary escape
      from the burning summer.
But at noon, the sun will rage her orange fire.

And many wandering colonial paths
      will find themselves
under the canopy
      of a cafe.

Yet some still stroll down weathered roads,
looking
      for trinkets.

Once vibrant souvenirs whose souls have bled away under the heat
will be displayed everywhere.
      Bracelets.
      Earrings.
      Grass woven baskets.
Stones from the Maya River, fashioned into blades.

Postcards and stamps will be sent to faraway homes,
where eagles

soar in the skies
and pelicans are the myths.

This Sunday morning, I wake with the dawn
and look over rooftops and asphalt streets,
To faraway islands and soaring seabirds.

I see drunken fishermen approaching the harbor,
And hear the sound of church bells,
disguised in a chorus of cawing gulls.

I turn away.

My mother is calling.

It's time for breakfast.

Awake by Caitlin Wire

What a waste to dream.
I suppose I could close my eyes
Run far afield
Taste a summer rain that falls all sweet
From the wings of jade dragons
That cut patterns in amethyst clouds
But I'd feel it fade with sun-song;
Solar sorrow at its loss would bleed me dry.
Instead, I could look into your eyes
Golden, neverending
Just
A moment
Longer

Hysteria by Tatum Liles

When my Mother told me he died the room immediately expanded
Yet I have never felt so suffocated
In a grief stricken panic
I tried to push the loving arms of comfort and consolation away
Almost as hard as my heart was trying to push straight out of my chest

"You're joking!"
Push them away
For if they do not console us
Then it is not happening
"You have to be joking"
Lay two hands on their chests and push them back.. back.. back
Do not give up just yet
Fight with every aching bone
"Please tell me you're joking!"
Don't stop
Do not let this new reality set in
If you fight hard enough
Yell loud enough
Push them back fast enough
Perhaps time itself will stop
"Get off of me!"
They step back
There is no one left to fight
Breathe in
Breathe out.
Become acquainted with the small pit now formed in our stomach
You lost the fight, and it has now found its forever home.

Entanglements and Decisions by Christopher Badroe

Shield your eyes from the reality of woe.
The complacency of age has made slow.
A spruce once from a seed has forgotten how to grow.
Work your body and mind to ruin, to rest forever in the earth below.
Your reflection in the mirror is not the person you know.

The Blue Jay Flys and the Koi Swims.
A broken man near death remembers only hymns.
A river that bent to him on a whim.
An indulgent life saturated in lust and sin.
Released a beast within, a succubus of his perfect twin.

Feel the fury of mistreatment deep, in your heart where it soundly sleeps.
Under the skin and into the flesh is where is seeps.
Another scar on the soul, a tally it keeps.
A silent alarm and no one hears you weep.
Either die or change, but one has to be complete.

A child does not mature from a parent's protection or love.
There is not a dove or siren from the heavens above.
A transfer of suffering from those beloved.
Mature those bore innocent, a song that cannot be unsung.
A verse for a man and a chorus for a beast.
The appearance of a priest, with a need to indulge and feast.

What is life without loss?
What is experience without cost?
Life hardens in time that which is inherently soft.

For life to use someone, they must be bought.
Before they expire and are thrown out to rot.

A fish suffocates on land while a man drowns in the sea.
Surrounded by the oxygen they so deeply need.
One can have all that they desire and that does not make them free.
Thinking you are outside because of the breeze.
When your locked in a prison, near the window, without a key.

Purpose is created by the soul and a dream.
To sacrifice one leads to extremes.
A culture of black and white, leave those blinded who have been blessed
with sight.
The undead unaware of their own demise.
Smile the brightest behind their hollow eyes.

Hands Held by Chase Martin

The first one was hard, maybe the hardest.
We saw it coming but the blow was unsoftened.
The elegance of the break disguised the omnipotent fracture.
The interrupted wave interrupts, the fracture breaks clean.
The first one was hard, maybe the hardest.

The second one was tragic, maybe the most tragic.
It surprised us in a way we thought we'd already been surprised.
The fracture fractures, the waves churning and frothing,
Using broken glass to salvage a mirror, our reflections distorted.
The second one was tragic, maybe the most tragic.

The third one was contemptuous, maybe the most contemptuous.
Ungraciously affecting, irrevocably tipping the scale.
A third ending for a book barely opened, each page turned after tedious.
Leaving us weary, wholly shattered,
leerily grasping for words to fill the blank page.
The third one was contemptuous, maybe the most contemptuous.

The three evolve into a singular weight,
horribly distanced from where we were.
But where we were could never be where we are,
ignorant of where we will be.

The fourth will come, to be sure, but I do not fear it nor am I jaded by
its enduring threat.
The weight of three link together like chainmail,
my armor delicate but fortified.

Hold my hands, as I hold yours, and know our hands are not alone.

For when I dream, I hold the hands of the three weights, they are too heavy for this waking life

Our hands together held, from dark to light and over again

Our holding hands beget holding hands that temporary as they might feel,

Will write together the next page, the mended mirror of imperfectly reflected grace.

At Sea by Caitlin Wire

In what I imagine
Was your first breath
You sighed a thank you to the room
You fell into
Again, I can only imagine,
But to me,
It seems that you were radiant
From that beginning.

You sailed forward,
Facing hurricanes, but only stopping
To wipe the sea salt from your eyes
As you wrapped your arms
Around the small creatures in your boat
Keeping them warm and dry
And singing thank yous to shards of sunlight
That broke the clouds.
It seems to me
You were a beacon.

As the winds roared, perilous,
Ever closer,
The creatures built their own boats,
As did I.
We watched you thank us for our strength
Thank your own sinking boat
For doing battle against the elements
You think we did not see it.
Imagine that.

It seems to me the last parts of you we knew

Were the thousand thank yous

You'd imagined were lost at sea

We gathered them in our nets

And threw them into the clouds

So that when it rains

You fill the room

They fall into

And we stay afloat

Sailing steady

Sending a thousand thank yous

Back to your home in the sun.

Lovers of the Early Millenia by Emily Brown

You cum and it goes up my nose and we both laugh.
I get drunk after graduation and you help me up and down the stairs.
You drive two hours here and back
just to lay with me on the world's worst mattress.
I tell you I'm transsexual and you promise to
pay for the surgeries even though you're broke.
(This means more to me than any affirmation my mother could give.)
You can be pessimistic and you can be mean
and I wouldn't take you any other way.
We are not our parents. Let's get married.

November 17 2001 by Caterina Dong

Sometime ago my dad opened his fi t and I tumbled out. He wished it was C-section. He wished it was cessation. He wished she could be loved like she was a boy. My mother split into 2001 pieces when I split through her. Since then, I have only collected 19 of them back. An astonishing fact is that I was born 8 lbs heavy and he hated her for it. Since then, my dad has been trying to love the littler things. So too have I.

Addicts Bible by Jason May

From day one most of us were written off, another survivor or victim in
the proverbial, long family tree
Of broken families, mental cases, alcoholics and addicts
Some- who's only remnants that remain
are just maybe a fleeting memory.......
Or a picture we burned........because of anger
Thrown into a world with no flashing light to guide the way
So young and only rubble and ash with to play
Calling great or great great grandparents ma or pa.....
Best friend was a dog......I loved that fucking dog so much....
Hiding in closets.....the addicts bible and gospel.......
Why the fuck did I have to hide?......
The addicts bible. HIDE!.........
No wonder why none of you could look me in the eyes
No wonder why none of you could look me in the face
No wonder why none of you could tell me everything will be okay
No wonder why none of you stood up and showed me the way
Because deep down inside.......you knew that there would be that day......
That none of you would be around and I'd be all alone
The dog that I fucking loved so much was taken away because our
fucking home......
Was ashes and rubble and I was left to fend for myself and not even
being grown.....
Because you all replied on......
The Addicts Bible....
Its been so long since you've all been gone!.....
The Addicts Bible....HIDE!..

Summers End by Caitlin Wire

It was hot that day

Sweat made river-bends down my legs

And the sky was grey

Too shy to wear her colors with your eyes so bright

You fixed them on me,

And asked me to be your girl

As if it weren't already stitched into the universe

Shaman by Lawrence Weiss

we weave cloth for our ancestors
to wear on the other side
where the temple of the dead
is lensed through
the eyes of a yaguar

a child in green
great in wisdom
guides the people in dreams
bringing water
to our deserts
so the people might eat

the earth is alive
and we, part snake and part fish
shall not perish
for we have always lived here
three times in ages of wolf and fish
my ancestors cried, laughed
and gave birth along the road
to llama, antelope, and worm
crawling, loping or running
to the great river
at the end of the world
along a road woven not of topsoil
but of dreams
colored strands of corn silk
dyed with the cotton and hemp
of eternity

On Breaking Limits by Harrison Sussman

Escape they say
Escape away, to the inside
Breathe inward and leave this place

So exalted are they,
Unfamiliar ghosts, unaware of themselves
It seems there are no mirrors to escape into

In the same way
No inward place remains
To breathe freely

Escape?
To a place as inaccessible as it is unbreathable?
Silence enthralls all within earshot

Until once again
The unsolicited repeats
With a familiar sway

So they say it again
- with a twist this time -

'Escape anyway'

Search Party by Kathryn Bryant

I don't know where you came from.

I was looking for so long
That I set the search party on myself
They demanded answers
What's wrong with you?
What are you hiding?

Then you appeared
You told the search party to step down
We didn't need them anymore
Yes, we had answers
But we owed them none.

We started to build
Bricks that had collected dust were given a place
We agreed to use the broken ones
So long as we were honest
So long as the other knew
The search party stayed away.

They kept their ears to the ground
They saw a crack and whispered through it
Their voices filled your head like smoke
What's wrong with her?
What is she hiding?

One day the cracks became too many
Though we were always honest
Though the other always knew
Our shelter wouldn't hold
It learned what I was hiding.

And so we parted ways.

Now I'm left to wander
Alone again but it's not the same
I'm so tired of their spotlight
I miss what we built, broken bricks and all
I'll send the search party after you
But I don't know where you came from
So I don't know where you went.

The Cathedral by Lillian Stroup

Cathedrals of grace stood strong under the night sky. Freedom screamed from mouths of gargoyles and rang true from chimes of faith. Scaffoldings rebuilding past pains gave hope to my soul. Let there be light through these liberated stained-glass windows. Watch sculptures smile as I walk past, a reminder that hearts made of stone will warm again.

Towers of laughter stood among the stars, reflected in your eyes. Clear waters of peace flow through fountains of your touch. A sacred garden blooms around this solid cathedral of worship, much like my flourishing faith in you.

Lead me to the chapel and dance with me among the pews. Twirl my skepticism around this altar, help me leave it in the crypt. Interlace your arm with mine as we sip holy water of newfound infatuation.
Lastly, take me to the cross at the end of this aisle. Wave your hand over it, turning the wooden statue into a symbol of infinity. For this is not faith in an almighty God,

This is faith in the power of us.

The Old Youngster by Herbert Uecker

Twas a bright sunny spot at a sidewalk café
Two lucky young brothers sat facing each other
Under the care of their lovely young mother
Eating their pizza in a most comical way
With bulging cheeks they squirmed and wiggled
As they tried to swallow, but mostly just giggled
A carefree old man came ambling by
As they looked him over with curious eyes
Catching their glances, he turned and blurted
"Is it good?" while he put on a goofy face
They almost spit pizza all over the place
Their mom tried in vain to stifle her mirth,
But finally grinned at the playful old boy
Doffing his crumpled old hat with a flair,
He bowed and left, smiling all the way home
He still lived there, gladly, yet sadly, alone,
He soon dozed off in his favorite old chair
And when in the morning they found him there
A smile still graced his cheerful old face.

The Head and the Heart by Hannah Collom

How many times have I wrote the same story?
The head and the heart are tricky.
They're deceitful.
And half the time, they are at war.
They're powerful enough to set fire to the world.
But we fall powerless to their desires, therefore, led by a losing battle of
the head and the heart.
So, gain strength over them.
But we don't know how.
And so, it is a constant suffering. A constant treading of water.
The head and the heart deceive themselves.
At what point the truth lies… I don't know.
Beneath the emotion, the logic, the hurt, the love, the empty corners –
we don't know what to
find, because it is covered indecision.
So, we grasp at anything.
Anything that makes us feel high – euphoric.
And because of that, you think you've found happiness, but what had
happened was you were
riding an unsustainable high.
One that leaves you mid-air, caught in a slight pause.
A moment to let you know that you're about to fall.
And it's violent. Unapologetic.
It is catastrophic if you don't learn how to grab hold of reality and steady
yourself on the way
down.
So, you crash.
You have to let yourself crash.

Completely fall until you are hit so hard with reality that you are forced to face it in the darkest
point of its being.
And maybe then, you'll find what the head and the heart never could.

The Hoods by Kristi Adams

Childhood.
Someone holds me lovingly. There is laughing. I see a statue in a cozy
Wisconsin dining lodge: "The monkey with the open mouth!"
Joy to instant VISCERAL TERROR. Uncontrollable sobs. None of us
know why.

Chicken pox. ITCHING. BLEEDING. A whole thumb nail lost.
Our bodies can be harmed, but suffering can be shared, laughed back
on together.

STICK INSECT!
This world has creatures actively trying to deceive you.
HOW DARE THEY.

"Tie my shoe?"
It's wrong, but some friends just do what you ask.

Wishes, prayers; asking for a guitar every night. Notes to gods and fairy
godmothers for a "compooter."
Magic is for movies, children.

Teenagerhood.
"I stayed at Molly's."
Provide an alternate narrative and get away with it. Dual realities exist.

Drops of LSD from a bottle.
Colors can CHANGE. If we try, we can see through playing cards.
Don't look in the mirror too much unless you're ready to see. I am the
God of ME!

Head butted. Falling, nose smash.
"THAT is the problem [pointing to the devil poster I just ripped on the gross music studio wall]. We are free when nothing matters.

"Derrrr, that's like, rape."
Airhead boys, too dumb to comprehend what they're accused of.

"I've been through worse…"
"LIKE WHAT?"

"Is Officer X______ here?"
Your actions could kill someone. Don't drive intoxicated –unless you want to hate yourself more.

Adulthood.
"Look out for my boy – hahaha!"
Parents can love you but like your partner more. Blood is not thicker than water, scientific bonds.

Sand below. A sudden hop up from a once teary-eyed man,
a kiss on my forehead.
You can give your abuser the best day of their life by "forgiving," years later.

"I do."
But you are not worthy of me. I shall slam you against the wall and push you down the stairs, because you like cruelty, right?

Study lectures. Books! A quiet, green place with monks.
A million miles away.
Dead of night, marketplace ablaze, hundreds of families' livelihoods lost. A beast beneath. The Monkey with the Open Mouth.

Dad drops dead.
At least I tried to end the silence. SHE DIDN'T ATTEMPT CPR. Did
she give him my messages?

East coast. A revised, humanitarian purpose. A severed refugee girls'
arm on a merry go round "we provided."
You are not part of a grand solution.

"I do"
"I most definitely do not"

PAIN. Cigarettes. Punk rock, beer, fairy lights. The best bear hugs.
Tender, warm.
What your heart always imagined? It's real.

Whats That Part of Me by Dominik Heliosch

I am a killer

I am a runner

I am tired

I shoot for the stars.

I feel lonely

I feel horny

I want to meet people

I wish I was alone.

I am a chiller

I am a party lover

I hate drinking

I can see the future

I was quiet

I was the star of the night.

When I think

And can't stop thinking

That what's me

Is not what I want.

But who I am

I can't change

So what is left

Is acceptance

For who I am

What I do

And what I don't.

The Pressure of the Earth Moving On by Bronwen Dingeman

I ask you now if it is debilitating or enriching to let a piece of prose,
poetry, song;
wanders its way behind the backs of your ears,
and whisper your own lonely truth back to you?
And then I answer for you:
It is both.
It is one thousand tender emotions.

It is lyrical time warps.
Cosmic intertextuality.
The descent into self.
Into hell.
Rhythm of blood.
The song of the stars and
scream of mankind.
When the human condition feels palatable,
and melodramatic yearning,
justified.
When aching with undefined longing becomes
defined again,
and the pressure of the earth moving on is holy.
When those futile shouts into the ether gather no response,
from a god or a universe which empathizes,
it is a companionship.
An ode to nothingness.
A plea to understanding,
of which you understand.

Immortalized and still,

these are the feelings that must happen to me.

Here, in my ears,

this poetry, this truth, this mouth-ful of decay.

It is both.

It is one thousand tender emotions.

Viet Everywhere by Brady Bowen

A man paces outside my bedroom door
not a plodding stomping ambulation
oh no
these are the softly lowered footsteps of
the cat you see, he hunts a version of himself that vanished while he
wiped an eyebrow
off of his face less than two minutes forty-five seconds on base because
Twentieth Century Fox didn't even have time to finish before a PFC with
the accent of Appalachia ate a sniper's bullet for breakfast and just threw
up everything on his crisp green. Even eyebrows.
Murmured discourse of battles gone
flow under my door like whispersmoke
Doc Tho, on alert, of course it's insane it's
The Nam, overrun, KIA MIA POW TOD
a hundred acronyms written in olive drab
it doesn't scare me now
I peeked last week
as he froze I froze heart hammering
but I instantly knew

I was safe if only
I don't enter Viet Fucking Livingroom
tonight.
Back into my bed I climb
he'll be quiet and somber in the morning
I'll awaken before everyone else
smiling as I walk into last night's war zone
and climb into his lap on his old recliner

he'll startle like an electric shock
heat lightning in bloodshot vigilance
then fold his arm around me
the house is silent but for the sound of
cool air flowing through aluminum arteries

a starling sings needle needle threedle nee
and though I am small in Viet Living Room
I feel invincible in the warrior's arms
until my sister cries Reveille.

A Conspiracy of Two by Tim McMahon

Two Ravens

(I am sure they would attack me if I called them crows)

(Or denied them a capital letter)

Have commandeered the tallest of the pine trees in my garden

They are completely black, of course, but a luminescent black

Almost blinding in an intensity that I would have thought impossible

Before (I hope they have come as guardians and not as omens).

Nor would I have believed that just two birds could make so much noise

For such prolonged periods

Shrieking and screeching at all hours

Even when all good birds, except owls and nighthawks, should be asleep.

And the size of them, colossal certainly, but epic is more exact.

So immense in substance and presence,

I am sure that if they don't belong to Odin

Then they belong to someone, or something, even more dangerous.

I hear local farmers have been granted a licence to cull.

I won't be joining them or letting them onto my land.

It would, I think, be very unwise to try and shoot these two.

I am happy to be their guardian, I hope they will repay the favor.

Bella Figura 5-2-12 by Ernst Hoyer

Today, we may be ready to consider, The way we live, the road we will choose. Is time just for the highest bidder? Could we escape from our own litter? Is there any solution; is there an excuse?

For what is time? Just an agreeing, in the way we measure: why are we? From about two hundred thousand years of being. With only twenty thousand years foreseeing, Whereafter Earth keeps-on spinning dazedly.

Humans and earth were once united, in their caring for animals and plants. But all of value is doomed to be blighted. Where space becomes scarce, it will be fighted, And every attempt to keep diversity, strands.

Source of our existence: water, Once a clear streamlet, now just a drain. The sparkling splashing of Zeus' daughter, has degenerated into slaughter, A withered well's what will remain.

The pure clean air, born with us together, gasping for breath now, is in distress. Soot and carbon do change the weather, The view on the horizon doesn't anymore matter, And the evening sun wears a blood red dress.

Deep dark nights, that made us craving, for fire, for light, a feel-safe spot. Now light has caught us through enslaving, Sirens' chants blocking our wills behaving. Darkness is conspicuous by being not.

The inexorable law sticks the species to the curve. A figure that grows, flattens and finally bends. The quintessence of our being is to dance; not to serve our genes, that either want progress or all to preserve. Because by the beauty of art, time never ends.

Another is Aimed by Jordan Coomer

Aimed. Hungry and tight-
a quiver-
then we are off with furious red hunger in the humid early labor heavy
wet work before staring wonder at the vibration, deafening reflection,
kaleidoscopic caressing over the smell,
warm metal and musty blanket. Fixin to sing high and quiet rhythm
the creaking porous wood which cradles, a glimpse of moon through
cottony veils and velvet night,
a white fire blinking behind the prehensile fingers of coveting wisteria.
The song is old.
In the muggy mornings the children walk without enthusiasm.
In the mornings, the bloodthirsty fevered mornings they walk and wait.
The clammy hands of time drag along the lines, seasons or memories.
Mark your time as you wish, but neatly. Mark your clammy time, choose
your medium and render.

The scent of orange is subjective. Deciduous beliefs and teeth are kept in
boxes, or bagged, or lost. Dead magic whispers along the path you know.
It follows rustling in the quiet but waits, mocks, turns along the paths
you do not know.
There are reasons to live, such as candy. Now go, walk the path you know.
While pinned and posing you may quiver.
Spastic little wings caught in spiraling rows may be raised or lowered;
you may dream.
You will dream, you will turn it in using numbered font and double-
spaced margin.
Smile. Nevermind.
In the stiff evenings, spread crisp like parchment,

the workmen talk and drink.
Hopes ghost along the parapets of their minds which, cold and stony,
are preoccupied with should-haves and oh-wells.
Gaze upon the pewter evenings. In the murmering firelight,
there is still time.
There is time to be a ladylove, or a lunatic, or both.
Time to be a mother or a whore. Or both.
Time to arrange your mildewed wishes out on the flannel in the firelight,
the splitting gossip of the fire.

There is a shadow that follows.
In your walk with Solomon
through sinuous roads and impotent gardens, it follows.
Questions are forgotten, debris in the catacombs.
Answers are released, bristles in the wind.
The shadow reaches its tendrils
drawing near with nothing strange or new.
Nothing strange or new as wind carries-
while hands sweep fevered heads.
While water copes, we plan or do
or nuzzle the cheek of Perhaps, but-
greedily blooming pink rises
in the leaf-dressed
sternum of Earth
until then-
another is-

Armor of Amour by Wei Yao

My love for you

      is not for you

My love for you

      is for me to enjoy

            for me to lay out under the honeyed sun

            for me to wrap around my tickled smile

My love for you

      is for me to imagine

            for me to compose an alluring masterpiece of us

            for me to indulge in a tipsy dream of eternity

My love for you

      is for me to inspire

            for me to face Cerberus in shining armor of amour

            for me to conquer Everest riding on my iron lionheart

My love for you

      is for me to suffer

            for me to butcher my raw bleeding being into pieces

            for me to hang my dismembered soul on biting hooks

My love for you

      is for me to live

            for me to serve my time for the grave crime of love

            for me to revive my breath after rising from death

            My love for you

                  is not for you

        My love for you

            is for me to remember

When my withered heart can no longer recall

                the tender arc of your distant eyes

Flowers of Her by Charis Barton

Flowers, all so enchanting- inspiring, meaningful. Each glows, each
dances with the breeze, and
each flourishes with the touch of tender soil.
For all that she is; blossoming. To what I cannot know, perhaps:
An Angelica? She whom inspires me with not a word.
A Freesia? As your trust unto me forever remains an invisible blessing.
A Peach Blossom, suits well unto me, for I know my capture,
indeed as I am lost.
An Alyssum? Describes my sight of you as it is impossible to ignore.
Indeed- my feelings for you I know, an Arbutus, a Red Crysanthamum
so obvious. Primrose.
You are a Coreopsis forever gleaming.
You are a Gladioli; strength forever presented, a burn inside your soul
that none can extinguish.
You are a Crocus; Joy in the new, cheerful in the adverse, humour and light.
A Red Tulip. An Acacia.

Bioluminescence by Tomader Ali

They told me you'll be there if I looked intently…deeply…don't be fooled by the shiny surface, they warned…do not
get swayed…
So I stayed…
I tried…softly…cold-water ripples greet my toes…stones move underneath…underneath my feet…getting…
adjusting…they've seen this before…
When the moon shines so brightly upon the murky waters…when fireflies know it is time to light the way…when
miracles seem graspable…when you feel most alone…watch your ask they told me…
The sky of blue to indigo hues.. are before me…the milky way galaxy on the waters lull me…lull me into their magic…
a bacterial soup of dazzle…a star in every drop…each drop a piece of my heart, each sparkle a tear of my eye, each
ripple a dream from my soul's stores…I watch them all drift…drift away into the glow…mesmerised…I stand frozen
…unable to stop the shedding…unable to save what was shed…
I wait in the silence…I want to scream 'I stand before you…what say you?…where are you?'…I hear nothing but
echoes at decibels that shatter glass…if only…if only that alone was the price…to break free from it all…alas…
Where is the line between a memory and a thought…a dream and a wish…where does my mind go when it cannot
open any more doors…You ask about life's rhythm and pace…for my feet know not of the steps they take anymore…
you ask where in the convoluted moments in time does my inspiration roam…well I watched it all float away in the

foam…the foam of those frothy murky waters that glow with want…
and fade with despair…the magic spirit will help
you…the magic spirit will come they say…but I see no man no spirit up
high by the moonlight behind the mountains
nor by the waters down below…how can one not believe their own eyes…
Keep looking they say…why sure, there is nowhere for me to go…
But they…do go…the ideas…that were thoughts…that were ideas…
that become thoughts and ideas all over again…
one chases after the other until their nuclear fission pops, bangs and
explodes…obliterates my sight and smacks my
senses to stillness…the stillness of saints…
Something drags me to center and align…come back to it…come back…
keep onto the quest…one idea until we
rest…that was the line I remembered best…
Out of nowhere…I see you…there you are…a moment of lucid connec-
tion…I truly see you and your contours…I
touch the light of your frame on which my fingertip tours…I run my
prints on the pool of your glittery glow…that tells
a billion stories…ones I certainly did not know… I see all that glitters
and shines…comes entwined…with the thorns
of the unknown…if I could just shape my hands to reach that which
calls…calls from beyond all the hisses of fate…
and the good fortune promises that always seem so late. My third eye
acknowledges you…for it lay dormant for
longer than I care…I see visions of pastel rain on arid land…I hear sweet
surrender of tired racing souls on
resurrected marshland…I taste sweet dewy content, like a tuneful sur-
vival big band…
I felt your inspiration hit me…sweet arrival…I felt air under my feet…
transcend…oh I do not know how…I stretch to

touch something…anything…but all I mustered, was a push…I pushed past your outline…right through space and

time…both yours and mine…

I felt you leave…oh no not again…

That premature loss engulfs the night in a cover of darkness…the bacteria, algae, fireflies and stars…all crumpled on

the inside walls of that blanket you hold…a blanket of safety, of magic, of truths you would unfold…but the darkness

ensues and I feel…smaller…lost in its infinite dimensions…

Silence greets my confusion…the missing glow compounded this haunted intrusion…did I miss my moment or is

there more to go?…do I wait in the darkness or will the man in the moon come back down like before?…

I'm awake, feet on the ground surprised by the cold stones…hairs raised…my skin bumpy and grazed…

You told me to look intently…and I did…don't believe your eyes…and I didn't…are my answers written in my blood

and you're testing me?…or is it ALL drawn on my face and you're… mocking…me?…

I came…desecrated…eradicated…it all seemed so…complicated… where did all your promises go?…wait for me, just

…wait for me…for I finally tasted…what my emancipated…self… might be…

Guilt by Amy Maina

Wracked with guilt, my life has been,
The guilt of my parents, my ancestor's seeds,
I am a monster, an ogre, lost to the fear,
The fear of my flaws and my failures are clear.

My love for you, it had turned sour,
The days that I spent, lost hour by hour.
I was lost in these thoughts that all would go wrong,
When really, it was only me singing that song.

I never meant for things to be this way,
All I ever wanted was for your happiness to stay.
Even when I should have known better,
The pain still won through, I should have done better.

Only your love has set me free,
It has brought to me this clarity,
You showed me that there is forgiveness inside,
No matter what I have done, there is no need to run, no need to hide.

The guilt hangs around me, eating away,
Whilst I try to carry on, living each day.
I must accept these awful things came from me,
Hurting my nearest and dearest, my innocent child.

But love lives on, and here it is to stay,
I feel like my soul is as bright as the day.
Melted away are all my great fears,
And all that is left, are my perfect dears.

Human Nature by Roberta Bassetti

Just like the plumbago
That always seeks the sunny side,
I want to see the best in you,
I want to know the kind, the gentle,
The even sentimental
Part of you.
And in Spring,
When we open and bloom,
I want to feel you flourish and shine,
Bring warmth to my winter soul
And even, I dare, be mine.
Give hope to my little sadness,
Spread joy to my every day,
Stretch my limbs,
Cherish my shoots,
Stroke my branches,
Watch me sway.
And in this garden of somewhere,
This world of you and me,
With your strength and, I like, confidence,
Your hand on heart truth time,
Your age and sheer experience
With my rhythm and my rhyme,
You will water me,
Sweeten me, care for me,
Be there for me,
And you know,
Yes, you know,
I will really be just fine.

I Am by Ethan Park

I am

A short Korean boy

A nerd, but not

Always moving around a court

Rehearsing to put on a show

Jumping and running from place to place

Energy to spare

Standing in the Oregon weather

Still moving for something more

Surrounded by all different types of people

Still being inspired by those around me

Pushed to greater heights, to greater limits

Multifaceted, like a shattered mirror

Sarcasm sharp enough to cut

Constantly taking Ls but still hoping for a W

I am Ethan

Only the Stars by Jose Mtz

As the stars shine
In the midnight sky
You appeared
A dream so surreal
Blanketed by the moonlight
Your hair, your skin
The way your dress fluttered
In the wind
Tortured my eyes
With their overwhelming elegance
As only the stars
In their infinite surroundings
Have phenomenally
Cast themselves to me

Passion Burning by Jonathan Morris

Where once a light shone brightly,
There is now only darkness and despair.
Where once warmth flowed,
There is only darkness and despair.

Where once was burned a great hot flame,
There is only darkness and despair.
No embers to be found, no sparks to be seen.
Only darkness and despair.

Pray! Pray! Pray! To the gods of fire and light!
Pray! Pray! Pray! For salvation from this night.
Strike together two souls,
Like flint upon steel.

Ignite the dry tinder,
Of my heart.
Take hold, little flame, take hold.
Burn! Burn! Burn! Little flame.

Shine your light upon the darkness!
Radiate your heat upon despair!
Burn! Burn! Burn! Little flame,
Set our hearts ablaze

Burn! Burn! Burn!
The darkness and despair.

The Bar of Chocolate by Kristen Porter

The purple packaging, the tin foil wrapped around the bitter dark chocolate
Filled with the sweet taste of caramel
The door opens, I move my eyes up and feel ice rush through my veins
Just as it does when I walk outside on the coldest days of winter
He stands with his blackened teeth, broken glasses, and valleys dug into
the sides of his face
I run to my room,
I lie down on my bed and break off a piece of my chocolate
As I put it into my mouth, I can taste the salt
Not from the caramel but from the tears now rushing down my face, I
just sit there and wait
To hear the screams of my sister
when I tell her he is back here in our lives, and in our house
Not lurking outside our windows in the middle of the night
Not barging in during our her graduation party
He is here and there is a black cast around my heart
I wait longer in my sisters' room, I wait at my phone to hear the poor
excuses from my mother
We rush to pack our bags and run out into the night,
only the moon guiding our way
I see the stiff grip from my sister hands on the steering wheel
I see the pools of tears drop down from her mortified face
As if someone dropped the weight of the world on the tip of her finger
Later to collapse into the arms of our grandparents, and then our sisters
While I wait with my sister, I imagine my mother's mind
As she fell into the same old schemes, same old games, same old cycle
I remember the look of the pink colored chocolate
and flowers on my birthday

Then the pink on my pepper spray and the color of my hands
To clinging to the handle like it was some kind of life force
I am done waiting and I'm taking my chocolate and wrapping it up
I'm leaving it for myself, for the family I choose
Not the people who forced me to leave the chocolate on my desk
But the people who help me make more and lay down their wrappers
For the world to see that not everyone has to let their chocolate melt

The Sun and The Moon by Calum Finlay

How many journeys made the moon unseen,
stealing o'er the celestial sheet as one,
until it found it's love in borrowed sheen
and joined in happy union with the sun?
The sun with one eye looked over all the world.
It's gaze went unmet by glassy human sight
until the moon inside that orb was furled;
a pupil to eclipse its fiery light.
Alone both sun and moon, life and tides made;
and winter's white was turned to summer's green.
But, in borrowing light and embracing shade
they allowed the other's beauty to be seen.

For when heaven's rings are wedded in the skies,
commingled light is glimpsed by mortal eyes.

The Talk by Sharnta Bullard

Did you have the talk with your kid yet?
You know the one,
the one that discusses
how to stand up straight,
look them dead in the face,
never let them catch you alone in a space.
How they will try to discredit you all because of your race?
No wearing hoodies.
No playing with toy guns,
and absolutely no clowning around for fun?
When you are in their presence,
never be caught guessing.
Always speak clearly
and appear non-threatening.
The talk to say
no matter what you do
the culprit will always be you.
The talk that rips their childhood away,
introduces fear,
the one you'll need to re-visit,
year after year.
The talk you rather not have,
but one you pour all your passion in as if it were your last.
The talk to teach them how to come home safe,
gets them through another day
and makes you question why the world has to be this way.

Treasure of Denial by Lakeshia Teel

Adjectives, verb, nouns, protruding from your lips is what I'm
so desperately missing now

The show is already over before it even started, so there's no need for an
introduction or a need to take a bow

A disturbing trend, complete insanity, the essence of nightmares,
looking for an exit route

By any means necessary, anyway and anyhow!

I must have glanced at my phone a million times,
searching for any presence of you,

Yet excuses are all that I find, and the magnetic hold that you
have over me, my body, and my mind!

I can't explain why I blocked you out of my life, matters of the heart
never seem to go right

It seems that love and happiness always battle it out and go head to head
in the ultimate fight!

I wonder if you're thinking about me, the way I'm thinking about you

And if you know that your words watered my soul and as a result
my confidence grew!

A real life portrait of Cinderella trying on the perfect shoe, with a cloud
of mystery and no clue

A heart so battered and bruised, a look of bewilderment in your eyes,
I know you're confused

With all that being said, I can't take my imperfections out on you!

The way your kisses stampeded the outside of my neck, left little for the
imagination and when your arms wrapped around me, common sense
and reason simply took a vacation

Not at all allergic to this electrical sensation,
even though I must ask you again to be patient

While we stand on the edge of this cliff,
looking into each other's eyes, our hearts racing

Reality is what I'm facing, but oblivion is what I'm chasing

Somewhere in a perfect world, our lives become entangled,
and our souls adjacent!

War and Women by Bronwen Dingeman

Women, women, women, and
little men;
how we terrify them,
with deliberate words and wicked whims.
We are willful and afraid of nothing.
Articulate, alluring, and annihilating,
prayer incarnates.

You walk in a meadow of adamant emotion,
that is neither debilitating or discrediting,
but fertilizing
the pastures of understanding.
Profound and blood-aching,
is the realization of this awakening;
That you may be reckless and graceless.
Terrifying or tender.
Whisper into ears and,
let your eyes blaze for the first time,
amidst your intimate,
empire-sized inner vigor.

Spit out the mess of yourself,
and refuse to be good and silent.
There is no language to describe,
the wit you speak in.
No sentiment to stain eyelids;
you could build pyramids,
with the effort it takes,

to stifle your tongue.
Cherish the humble and lustrous life.
Treasure the soil and the terror beneath it.

You were grown to hurry half-dressed,
barefoot in the grass,
and scream at the flowers;
exclaiming their dearness.
Their honey-eyed heaviness is of resemblance,
to your lush eagerness,
to be wild and lovely for a minute.
How ironic it is,
When you were born as both
War and woman.

After the Funeral by Elena Apanovitch

Grief like water through my fingers
Winter light encased in silence
Fading sunlight
Glowing embers
Longing trapped in trembling eyelids

Those who stayed and those who parted
Ways in search of absolution
Wistful whispers
Windless spaces
Incandescent vows receding
Folded hands on cooling linens
Nothing left but patient waiting

Time of timeless explanations
Truths revealed by deeper knowing
Farewells and separations
Held in place by embers glowing

Amanita by Madalyn Chevalier

Speak to me of the earth's strange and macabre.
I no longer wish to hear
of dancing butterflies
and whispering leaves
or of sunny daffodils and babbling brooks.
No.

Speak to me instead of mushrooms
contorted and pungent
who tip their poisoned caps
to the beatles and the worms
with whom they make their home.

Speak to me of the bats
who shun the happy rays of sun
who would rather navigate the night
blind and screeching their way
with pushed in faces and beady eyes.

Speak to me of the snakes
who slither acid green
through dried leaves and splintered wood
with slitted eyes and sharpened fangs
they stalk the forest floor.

I have had my share of sunny days,
of dandelion wishes full of hope
I want to speak of the damned.

A Pact By Pound by Calvin Borghardt

A Pact by Pound pronounced:
Whitman broke the new wood.
"Now is a time for carving."

Yet I remain dead wood,
Adrift in an aged world,
Overseas through these seasons.

I can't recall my reasons,
All these shadows whose shade
Sparks my revelations.

As questioner or quester,
I cannot tell myself:
"I am my own successor."

Thus I lit a live flame
For dead wood from that old world
And ignite this bard's shame.

After funeral pyres praise,
A stack of smoke barks a haze
And their fires torch my form.

Darkness dims diminished
With this corpse cremated
And created my carving.

Blue by Jo Gardiner

We painted our lips with berries, and wandered along
the kurumes, a glass in hand, to Bach's Cello Suites
and the end of the score.
The moon turned its golden ear and listened;
 the koi carp, half-asleep beneath the moon held her breath
and listened to a magpie workshop the night and give himself away
to one long note that erased uncertainty,
then fly into the gingko tree. Leaves slipped down onto silver-
skinned pods of yesterday's rain, and the sasanquas released
their scent like wrens scattering.
As the night drew on, the moment lengthened;
a strange hum flew between earth and the outer galaxies.
The obscure moon, its cool fire burning, travelled to the edge
of blue dusk running wild across the mountains
while all around us shadows flowed.
Stars budded in twilight and lit the gleaming skin beneath
your eyes—not to mention your eyes—and the bowerbird's
heartbeat became
the metronome that set the tempo
for our turquoise days. That first night in the wooden house,
your scent of oak moss, the sweet decay of books. The honey
wall, understanding our purpose,
carried our light within it.

Background by Musa Turner

there's two ways to see the black border
of a framed painting and the distinction
doesn't matter to most at a cafe,
breakfast pressing liminal thoughts down hungry heads ,
a discount bouquet on an empty highway
one piece meant to subtract from another in order to
reaggravate the most important spaces with serotonin.
they don't mean nothing in the grand scheme of a presentation
that lingers where you used to be able to trust your gut,
a body given two guesses and then a third
before the question stays open, empty.
it's weird to say something supports the unknown
or vice versa but in silence it makes perfect sense
repeating an incantation of good lucks and lullabie
s who knows how many times
before reappearing in between canvas and culture,
in no clearly particular order
swinging, in the way that a hungry person imagines
 a fruit firmly attached to a tree
as they build a basket below, hoping for it to fall.
there's something beautiful in waiting,
and the way it cares for all parts of an
infant and everlasting space,
preparing to tear borders in order for full bellies
with something to share to do so smoothly
that or it's nothing worth talking about
in the way a pristine street is modest and an unmarked

parking garage screams in every direction.
the edges tell the story of an unseen ending
and only those loving enough to embrace a cliffside
have imagined its most true ending.

Cold Soup by August James

The poor wretch,
forced into a filthy dark corner.
Apologize, you coward, lick his boots. Beg for mercy.

Please, please, don't hit me anymore!
The soup was cold again.

Ripped from the table,
the bowl explodes on the wall above me,
broth splatters the wretched thing.

Little pieces of my soul breaking across the floor,
joining the broken ceramic dish.
The soup was cold again.

I don't laugh anymore,
or smile.
That part of myself was lost,
or stolen.

Please, please, don't hit me anymore,
I'm sorry the soup was cold again.

Compassion by Beth Bolton

Compassion
turned her tears
into roses.

Compassion
gave her strength
like a lion.

Able now
to protect herself,
she stood strong.

Facing the troubles,
water transformed
to petals.

Glitter bursts!
So sweet off
that thorny vine.

pink, red, purple;
nothing now
feels impossible.

Compassion
turned her tears
into roses.

Cross Winds by Barbara Olsen

The cold perfection of the belligerent wind rallies

above our heads, marking an end to our solitary days.

Deep in the sagebrush thicket the hare's heartbeat jumps,

a quickening, an upending of the delicate three-year marriage

between a breath of air and the crisscross crannies of the alveoli.

Sensing an opportunity, a tarantula crawls slowly from under its rock,

never thinking its last breath imminent, lest at the hands of a death adder.

Whilst we struggle to puzzle out the New York Times crossword, suddenly

the wind stops blowing, those labyrinthine words now etch indelibly across

our stelae.

Diamond by Bianca Leigh

Her shine is blinding. Her corners and lines perfectly crafted and shaped just for my satisfaction. Her hug is not filling, but it's home to me. If I were to lose her I know the pieces of who I am would disintegrate and come to nothing. When I feel I've had enough of her I find that I haven't even discovered half of her. There is much of her to uncover that is why she can never be hidden. In my darkness she is my first look at light. Beauty and Purity is what you may call her if you are permitted to obtain her.

First Words by Win Anderson

I recall sitting engulfed
by an old multicolored
blanket, carved by some ancient
hand. Whittled of yarn,
stitched of time. Probably,
the sculptor was blind.

I remember diffuse light
as at dusk or dawn.
This light felt musty,
sort of winding
down not building up.

And speaking, I was
speaking. Referencing
some feathered creature
perched in time.

Then, a great while later
I wrote down this memory.
So that it would not

forget me.

Flutterby by Barbara Olsen

How do we (h)arm our children then
with logic and the commonest of senses
when the world around them is anything but logical
       and
           sensical?
Forest fires are caused by Jewish space lasers designed
       to replace
           coal and oil
       (while we stand ankle-deep in the ashes of our ignorance)
School shootings are staged by child actors
       to garner
           anti-gun sentiment
       (while we watch construction paper pines
F l u t t e r B y
       in the aftermath of the gun's
           re —
coil
       their twinkling crimson lights commingling
       with the spilled blood of our children)
Death threats are invoked by *patriots*
       to silence
           another mother
       (while we count on one hand the matriarchs in the mobs)
       We call heroes *cowards* and cowards *heroes*
and wonder if a single prideful boy held his son tight that morn
       whispered gently in his ear
           it's all going to be okay — I got this
before he closed the door and walked away.

Intuition by Bianca Leigh

It always comes true. I wish it wouldn't. One wrong move brings invites one raised eyebrow and one absurd thought. Intuition is a friend you'd never want if you don't socialize with the crowd of the estranged. It's like dipping your hand in a pond of mercy waters. Your shot in the dark became your reality, Now you must lift your wounded heart and move it onwards.

Once a Lily by Clyde Hopper

Once a lily, now a rose,
Transformation, head to toe.
Neither sage nor scholar,
Just the license to change,
Earth and universe, revolving, evolving,
Moving us closer, rearrange.

Rise to the best of us,
Manifest virtue, manifest trust.
Knowing who we love,
Knowing all we touch.

The raven lives in us all.
So to the hummingbird, falcon, and kestrel.
The dark is shaped by light.
So too the blind by sight.

Once the captive, now the free,
Incarnation, reality.
Neither cold nor callous,
Just the curve of a blade,
Road and roadblock, humbling, crumbling,
Building us up, crusade.

The Death of a Procrastinator by Bruce Ru

I am a child, so
I have time.
A long life stretches in front of me.
Let the clock tick.
I don't need to do anything right now.

They say I am an adult now, but still,
I have time.
Job opportunities are everywhere,
And I have decades to be a millionaire.
I don't bother right now.

Since when was I a middle-aged man? But still,
I have time.
It's never too late to start a family.
And as for that trip to Europe?
I don't have to go right now.

Wrinkles weave my face now, but still,
I have time.
Who cares about having grandchildren?
I could again be that merry child myself
If the clock agrees to tick back a little bit right now…

Rest in the Sky by Catrinna Sjoblom

Sometimes I have this dream
That you are next to me
We're driving through the countryside
On our way out to the sea
Rolled down windows letting in
The smell of salty breeze
The warm summer sunshine
Peeking through the trees
Happiness upon us
Laughter fills the air
It's always nice to see you again
And feel like you're still there
Alas when morning wakes me
For again you disappear
Back into the heavens you go
But I'll always love you, dear

The Narcissist by Bronzy

It hurts that I am hurting you
The narcissist he cries
And a tiny snippet dies inside

As it dawned she realised
The twisted words
That look like truth are lies
And not at all re her demise

But all about his own reprise
And worming out of compromise
And conflict
And all empathy
And all responsibility
Until there's no strands tenuously
To see
Tee hee

Oh clever clever me me me, he he he, hee hee

The Pleasure Point Magic Myth by JC Gordon

The Pleasure Point created themselves in order to come alive
While humanity exists merely to confirm you survive.
We live in darkness and require Your touch
To blind the dragon through Thy crutch.
So one can be All and All can be one
Here, my life has just begun.
Do it Now, Do it Now.
Do it-Do it-Do it.
Yes!

Yes!
Do it-Do it-Do it
Do it Now, Do it Now.
So my life will have just begun
And One can be All so All can be One.
We blinded the dragon through Thy crutch
And ended its darkness that required Your touch.
Now, humanity will have confirmed that you survive
The Pleasure Point created themselves only to come alive.

Traveler by Carlos Avitia Velazquez

Listen, Traveller: while you're young,
Be not too quick to do as told.
For if you're bold, I promise you
You'll live a life worth more than gold.

It may seem hard to trust yourself
When vast horizons sprawl ahead,
But heed me, Traveller: you'll regret
Not going where your soul directs.

The rigid routes may be well-tread
(And safer than those unmarked roads),
But leisure is a consequence
Of dreams renounced to pay the tolls.

It's true, you'll reach your journey's end
Less worn and scarred than "Fools Who Tried"–
But souls that burn with wanderlust
Cannot be quelled with tempered lives;

The flame that flickers deep within
When you look back upon your days
Will haunt you in your twilight years
With embers of "What Could Have Been?"

So, Traveller–be not afraid!
I promise you it's worth the cost,
For even when storms find you lost
Your dreams you'll never have to vend–
And thus you'll triumph in the end.

A Beautiful Nuisance by Ato Dankwa

Another reason for striving to attain my goals;

Another spark in the darkness that restores my soul;

Another factor to consider when all seems low;

Another light in my life that deserves to glow;

Another wish at night for sweet dreams to sow;

Another beat in my heart that I care to grow;

Yes, a beautiful nuisance (being loved), I know.

xo

When You Least Expect it by Caroline Jacob

We seek love and find it in the least expected way,
It was a union willed by all and we wanted it to stay,
There were many things to say, some needed some not,
We knew it wasn't going to be easy,
But deep down we knew, this was not right or wrong,
We felt somewhere we did belong,
Looking back at that moment,
Something felt different, something felt good,
It's true what they say, sometimes love is all you need,

Geronimo by Kelly Conley

Geronimo,
The sacred name across the lands.
In the Wild West, the medicine man roams,
To the beat of the drums that no one knows.
Geronimo,
The paratrooper's war song.
In the skies so high, you could hear the echoes of battle cries,
Like bomb shells shattering on the ground.
Geronimo,
Falling for you, burning for you.
In your eyes I can feel pure bliss, sheer happiness.
My battle cry, my love lullaby,
Geronimo.

Wild Indigo by Kris Bracewell

They were my best friend
Every up and down shared
Days spent laughing
Nights spent talking
I fell platonically in love with their glow
They were the wild, I was the indigo

But then came a boy
A seemingly nice one
I always knew the risk
The risk of him taking them away
But I fostered their relationship anyways

In their absence I realized
Were they really the one
Or did I fall in love with the idea
Of caring for someone
While I got nothing in return
But "laughs" and "fun"
It was a daydream
Stuck on a loop
One I fell for day after day
Never waking up to the true dismay

Now I am healing
Sad but healing
Creating a new circle
One that truly cares

And doesn't use me for my abundance of love
That I am eager to share

Remember my readers
You are worth more than one peer
Don't throw your energy
Into someone not mentally there
Instead, use your energy
To help yourself grow
And watch yourself blossom in the sun
You will be a beautiful flower, a wild indigo

You Two Are So Cute by Janie Jay

our journey is filled
with candies and cakes
red roses and flowers
forget my mistakes

all pamper and warmth
as I hold you close
I'll burn you and hurt you
but I love you most

Alive in Thought by Sana Mashadi

Do I falter underneath the sky?
Should I hunch my body so
heavily over the ground?
Am I weighed upon?
Like the bag that carries the soil?

Every moment in the car felt like a sentence
from a children's picture book.
Every shop I passed was an illustration –
every icy raindrop happening upon the
windshield a reminder of myself, myself, myself;
unreal, yet alive in thought.

I want to take off in epic flight,
and ruminate upon the land I depart from
(until my very last breath comes out as a
relieving sigh of lingering sentimentality).

Picture this: I am taking flight.
The wind numbs my fingers,
the sky gently touches my face.

A Way Hard Fall by J.M. King

I soaked these hands of mine in pools of blood,
Letting the color take to my fingertips—
When I saw something tender within reach,
I couldn't tear my hands from my chest,
I just let it slip through the cracks.

It seems I just can't help but
To throw myself at ledges,
Blissfully unaware of the railings I lean on—
Angels have fallen for less,
Yet I'm dying for more.

My eyes tend towards the ground—
They hadn't mentioned the long way down
When they offered me the spot on this pedestal.

A life Worth Telling by Savannah Morris

Do not dread the pain.

My darling, pain is how you know.

You have lived a life worth telling.

You broke cycles.

Changed lives.

Loved.

Laughed.

Cried.

Laughed until tears fell.

Pain is proof.

That life is everything we could ever dream of.

And, so much more.

Baby Buzzey by Jennifer Lieneck

Good morning, Baby Buzzey, the day is brand new,
So zip up your stripes, stretch your stinger out too.

Good morning mommy, please tell me a tale,
All about me and how bees will prevail.
This story is my favorite, it makes me feel bright,
Please tell me again, it is such a delight!

Baby Buzzey you know I'll tell you again,
How when you were born, you'd be the one to defend;
Our title, our crown, I knew from the start,
You'll one day be a queen, loyal and smart.

Your new life began in the tiniest egg,
A nurse bee took care of you as you got legs.
You ate lots of jelly, till you got wings;
Arms to work hard with, and a stinger that stings.

Mommy lays hundreds and thousands of bees,
Each one supporting the flowers and trees.
If they nurse, if they forage, or work as a drone,
Together we nurture our beautiful home.

One day, baby Buzzey, you'll eventually see,
Everything we do makes honey as sweet as can be.
A queen is strong, and smart, and powerful too,
I can't wait to see what the world has for you.

I love you mommy, thank you for our story,
I hope I can be strong like you in your glory,
I love you baby Buzzey, and whatever you become,
I'll be proud, because I get to be your mom.

Because of you Buzz by Azhari Jasman

Make it stop my boy pleads as he lifts one
       finger to point at the moon-glow how it
appears to be caught in a bee-chase with the
       bus we're entrapped in while another finger
he touches my knee with to keep up his poking *You*
       know we tried once I tell him and as his fingers
stop I find them laced beneath his chin a sign to
proceed with daddy's story-telling Once

half a century ago the strongest country in
       the world sent up above the strongest rocket
known to men and in it there sat three strong
       spacemen they gave the strongest one with
the strongest arm a flag-pole to dibble in the
       moon's rock-soil in hope of stopping this exact
phenomenon so my boy asks who came
       out next after Mister Strong-Arm I say *Buzz*

Aldrin He says *See, that's why!*

Disillusioned Beliefs by Samantha Meddaugh

You perceive me as extremely disabled.
I'm skilled, talented and beyond capable.

You look and say I'm hopelessly unfashionable.
I prefer plain, neutral to be more manageable.

You view me as a darkened, ugly smear.
I want to be regarded as your fellow peer.

You call me a recluse who is all alone.
I'm someone who likes to stay at home.

You assume me to be helpless and indigent.
I'm quite handy and diligent.

You consider me a bumble and weak.
I'm merely humble and meek.

You imagine my darkness to be full of strife.
I'm very adventurous with my life.

You discount that I don't have rights.
I'm a mentor, advocator, one who fights.

You devalue me as though I'm faceless.
I'm a cherished jewel that's priceless.

You disrespect, belittle and bully.
I deserve to be treated fairly and equally.

You act and claim to be superior to me.
In an instant you can be in the same boat as me.

Hive Demise by Daniel Moreschi

Where craggy rocks and oaks weave latent thrones around
The floral avenues; where jeweled grains are found:
A setting to precede the crowning of a queen
Of black and yellow serfs that buzz above the ground.

Yet homing-hums and gliding dances in-between
The sugary circles of petals, once part of their punctual routine,
Are merely memories. And the lonely, sparse arrays
Is a pressing cause to mourn patrols no longer seen.

Despite their plight, their regal realms are turned to frays
For sights and sounds of steel jaws and scything sways:
A trail of desecrated homes, both honed and holed,
Whenever human hubris forges baneful ways.

On other fronts, they fall in fields they helped to mold;
They're martyrs for the harvests and fruits that they uphold,
While crops are propped to rise like golden waves, yet wreak
Regicide through pesticides, that run along each bladed fold.

And all the while ceaseless carbon emissions continue to leak,
The final colonies can not withstand the cauldron's peak,
So rendering the fostered swathes of growing—sown
Of hasty seeds—to perish in a strangled streak.

The tragic end of their hives is a trigger to atone
For this tilt out of the timeless balance, our own.
With Mother Nature's feeding-chains soon overthrown,
We beckon stings, enter seasons dark and unknown.

How long Can a Body Hold by Phoebe Colby

How long can a body hold
its water before
flotsam jetsam
swim the reef trundled
good fish at the grill where
he popped a gill

How long can a body hold
the reverb infinite and
clean breaked compartments never
to shatter, matter -
switching right lane left
sans mirror

How long can a body hold
itself solid, stolid
before peaks break even to
stutter, shuttered between
glimpsing shades as she
chokes on utters of her
glancing gory pain

How The Rot Spreads by Khadija Koubaa

My mom once asked me what was wrong with me,
How on earth I ended up in such a state.
The answer to that question resides deep between my bones,
Woven so tightly around my scabrous ribs that it's hard for me to answer.

What haunts my soul the most is myself.
Yes, I am my own tragedy,
I am the butcher and the knife and the sheep waiting for slaughter.

It has become obvious that I revel in self-inflicted misery,
how I stab the flesh and lick the blade.
I have always been this way,
Fragile chaos, tender disaster.

I jump from high buildings and throw my hands into the fire
then cry about the pain.
I dig my nails into my flesh and tear at my skin,
then come whining about exposed meat

I developed this habit when I was only a child.
It seems some part of me came out twisted,
came out crooked, came out wrong.

How terrible, how strange, that I've grown so distorted,
when all I've been through
doesn't amount to anything close to what
could've left me in such a state.

My soul is a puzzle and half the pieces were lost on the way.
There are holes inside of me,
Blank spots lodged between organs and arteries.
In them, flowers never bloomed

I was told that nature hates the void,
so I took it upon myself to fill the gaps.
I buried in them the corpses of my childhood,
the torn limbs of my loneliness,
the rotten leaves of my failures

I cover my masterpiece with dirt and mildew
Then stitch my skin back into place
I thought I'd be finally full,
But I've never felt so hollow

That's how I discovered that the rot spreads
Yes, the rot spreads. So slowly, so carefully,
You barely feel it lacing itself into healthy organs and unscathed veins,
Killing everything in its wake and deepening the crevices.

I have more holes to fill now,
I don't know what to put in them anymore.
I simply toss in the rubbish
and hope flowers bloom from the dead lands.

To be filled with rot is better than to be empty.

My body is used to it by now.
He no longer tries to sate the macabre craving for self-destruction.

He has become a mere witness,
watching me set myself on fire and hungrily devour the flames.

And when slumber begrudgingly claims me,
he bends forward and picks up the pieces, or what remains.
He sews them back together with the golden thread of my mother's voice,
and the sturdy ropes of wishes that had not yet decayed.

It looks wrong. What was broken will never be the same.

My body steps back,
watching with sorrow the remnants of the massacre.
He's a deft craftsman, my body.
To give the hideous uniformity,
to make the half-dead seem alive.
That in itself is a kind of art.

He whispers, weary and breathless yet undefeated:
The blood red poppies of youth will see the spring,
for those who hibernate are not yet deceased.
The disease may have the soul,
but I won't let it take the body.

Lacrimosa by Killian Thompson

A calm-seething mass of blood and organs, full of hatred for the world.
A very, very sick black dog on a chain, emancipated.
Barking at nothing because the ringing never escapes its wretched, weary head
Begging for nourishment before devotion, biting any hand that dares feed it.

A mother's grief consumes me.

A very, very sick black dog would lie utterly still,
'Nay, his chest heaves wearily
He breathes the way a machine on the verge of devastation does;
There is a hissing from somewhere inside.

Poor puppy, pitiful puppy,
Grieve this living breathing thing, it has no time left
Don't get close to children, don't let go of Mommy's hand.

Small dying black dog on a hill.
Lacrimosa.
A small, insignificant death.

A mother's grief consumes me.

Nothing rises from that rotting body
Nothing bled out of it but fat and oil
Breaking down, feeding the grass beneath.
The dog doesn't rise.
Nothing good becomes of this.

A mother's grief consumes me.

Kentucky Dog by Nancy Bruce

After leaving my northern city to seek a southern home, I'm traveling way down south passing bluegrass horse farms. In a bourbon distilled land, there are fiery sunsets over lakes, lined with dancing goldenrods, fenced along hayfields of wild turkey. "So much richness in this land." A quiet stillness found only in a dream, but within my journey and all to take in, I discovered there is a heartbeat of a dog that's never completely seen. Some you'll pass on old porches or simply running free, others with their freedom of choices; settling on a forlorn attempt to be noticed, lying in the middle of a sun soaked country road.

Sadly, their kept like cheap souvenir stones, briefly admired, tossed aside and forgotten years ago. "This isn't a pricey purse dog on their way to a spa." But a mud-caked, dried pawed canine working hollers and hills. Amongst neighboring shots of double barrel guns, rooster stirring winds, their howls are heard over cattle, speaking; "True Warriors!" Summoning- "True Grit!" Howling an ancient song.

"Oh- They're a poem to write." "A song to remember." "A velvet childhood memory." "If only you'd see?" "They are everything that's Real." "Everything you'd wish to be."

Born outside, tied like prisoners to dirty resin homes, these weary soldiers survived weathered storms. "So strong, even a brave man needs a steady hand to fire and crawl dirty trenches." "A dog of this nature follows out into enemy line."

An old friend always holds true.

At the bottom of the backroad, you'll faithfully find; a mere country dog coiled in the sun.
"Carefully slow down as he looks you in the eye." Only broods of racing roosters desperately panic to cross in every direction. "He'll remain still."

A Kentucky Dog never forgets.

Lately, I've Been Thinking by Lilly Conducy

Lately, I've been thinking,
What if we had been born in each other's times?
If you had had my upbringing, and me yours?
Oh, how your world would have turned out.
Such a strong, smart, independent like yourself, in an open,
affluent, and loving environment.
In a time when you would have only been further encouraged with each
passing year,
Gaining more experience with every endeavor.
Certainly, you would not be where you are today.
But rather someone who others knew and respected,
with a continuously gaining audience.
Your words would be spoken by many, and your thoughts a starting place
for even more.
You would not be trapped in the world you live in today.
Instead, you would rule your own life with a skillful hand.

But that would really all be hinged upon me.
And based off what I have done in this life,
Your life might not even be obtainable.
For though you could handle both appearances,
It seems, I cannot even handle my own.
And so, the question again emerges.

Would you even have been able to be born in my place?

And, from the look of things down here, probably not.

For what I have done with my current life,

I would certainly have achieved even less in yours.

So, while you would have shined and become one for the history books,

Your life would have been lost in my own misunderstood idea of how life is to be pursued.

Thus, ending with only me, because I am your opposite,

Only reading the history books, nothing more.

Little Poem by Chris Butler

I am a little poem,
made, not born,
alone on this canvas
vacant of black ink,
a creation of mother's
nature before it is
buried along with her other
rough scrap paper drafts,
as a blizzard of snowballs
accumulates in the recycling bin
until the inevitable avalanche,
when all poetics melt
out of the pen's end.
But with too many
words to write,
there is only so many
empty pages of white.

Purple Thread by Kaylee Gibson

Scavenging for memories lost, she prowled the streets, woolen in black. A spool of thread fell out her pocket, purple, trailing behind her. She found a small letter beyond the waste basket that held in it a proposal. A business proposal of sorts. She grabbed it and hid it in her pocket. She asked a man for spare change. He had 50 cents. Pools of light lit her eyes, and a tear drop formed. It fell to the ground, amongst the rubble, where a young homeless woman lay. She turned around and grabbed the string of purple thread. She decided to follow it. She followed it until she reached another plain, of golden fields, like the woman's eyes. She saw into the future. 100 years from now. Where stone buildings from the Middle Ages had turned to dust and glass buildings towered to the heavens. She saw the purple string turn into fields of forests. Forests of the future. She saw a million stars form, and returned to look at her hands. She was still alive. She hadn't eaten in 7 days. She saw herself older. Dressed in a business suit of sorts. She was drawing a plan for the future; to house the forgotten.

She collected memories of those who had been left behind. Strung along. Outcasts, forgotten deities, libertines, the wounded, smashed cans of sardines hit the ground. A child grabbed them, and bit into the salt. Anything to satisfy the craving of hunger. A moment later, the clock chimed. The woman woolen in black collected the spool of thread. And all that existed, including time, gathered with it, and collapsed into her pocket. And with that, her, too.

She Forgot to Dream by Kiane Parham

Praying was going to save her life

Praying is what was going to make her a wife

She did all that praying and fell on her knees

Her mother told her to trust, obey, believe, and dream

She was surrounded by people who love her and the Holy Ghost

At hard times He was the one she needed the most

Being a sweetheart took her across the world

We will be women and we won't always be girls

The grace of God and all He blessed her with made her an achiever

All the things her parents filled her head with made her a diva

She followed her heart because the heart is where our journey begins

She watched out for her enemies but she spent time with her friends

She watched children make it out of the ghetto and become whatever they wanted to be

Even though they were near thugs and gangstas that wanted them to be as bad as they could be

Her mother told her to trust so she told the Lord everything

Her mother told her to obey so she treated her father like a king

Her mother told her to believe so she believed life was going to be good

Saying no to I can't and yes to I could

She moved out of the house, got rich, and became a queen

She did all these things for the Lord, her people, and her mother, but at the end of the day she forgot to dream

The Briefcase by Claire Taylor

A little kid on the porch swings
The kid has turned into a grown-man
Off to work with a suit and lunging a briefcase
filled with dreams, promises, opinions
from
other people

He carries this
until it falls at a bus station
the words like paper blow away in the wind
as this man hurries to clutch, seize, grasp
the words that feel
true to him

Like a flock of birds, the papers take flight
But the man crumples under the weight of what he just lost
He is picked up and thrown on the bus
paralyzed in darkness
He cannot see any light
He hears the whispers of other people pushing him on a path
He tries and tries to switch on the light that once shone in him
But the lightbulb is
out

He waits for something, anything, or anyone that may give him a jolt back
But the reality he thinks he knows is only the reality made by everyone
but himself

The Charcoal Flame by Ameera Khurram

All my life, I have been denied.

Disowned, disgraced, and deprived.

My skin color has stripped me of opportunities and chances.

Standing out among the masses.

And while you stand safely on the ground,

We are tossed into the hungry waves of the sea until we drown.

And while you bask in the glow of the world's spotlight,

We are shunned away to wither in pure darkness.

Worthless

But somewhere inside this inky pool of misery, there is a spark.

Adding to the kindling, ablaze in my heart.

Those hurtful words they spat at me feeding the flame.

Growing wilder, raging harder, until they are no longer tame.

Shifting, shrouding, snaking.

What emerges is fierce and bold.

This time, the fire isn't red or gold.

The Charcoal Flame, no doubt

  You want me silenced, left unspoken.

And though you will try, I won't be broken.

We all walk on the same ground.

We share the same planet, wrapped in clouds.

Yet, we have let our pride build walls of division.

Walls so tall and thick that they have obscured our vision.

So all people of colors and characters shall come together,

the only solution.

To watch these walls burn and build a substitution.

A New Revolution

Sometimes, we must let things perish to let something betterrise from the ashes.

Together, we will heal, sealing our wounds, cuts, and gashes.

While tongues of white-hot flames flicker, black ones will dance with them, too.

And our beliefs will stand solid and true.

Let us forget about our past prejudices, judgements, and greed.

For all that matters is the way we lead.

We have been blinded for far too long.

But each of us matter, we all belong.

Stay strong.

The Cruel Flies by Caleb Kliewer

What fat fabulous lies
Sprinkled with tiny truths
Glaring bits of wisdom
Mixed with tales of madness
But not from God
Unless God is a paradoxical person
No, persons
Of righteousness and lies
A dictator lording it over the flies
While sentencing them to die
Buzz here buzz there
From this shit to that shit
Fearing the web some book calls hell
Except hell hardly exists
In the nothingness of nothing
Or even in that ancient text
Unless
The flies who are cruel
Imaginative
And cunning
Put it there
So we interpret or reinterpret
(Depending on the mood)
Funny, dusty words

Left by flies who thought they would never die

In a language

More dead than those false friends

Who wrote them

And we call it the one true religion

Flies telling flies how to live

How to die

Spinning our own webs

Becoming spiders, yet remaining flies

Becoming gods, yet remaining apes

With big brains, and shaking fists

The Flashlight by Stephanie Woodman

I find myself in the dark and I am afraid.

I reach for my flashlight and, with relief, turn it on.

I am in a room that I have been in before.

Why am I afraid?

I remember being afraid of the dark as a small child.

My small child days are now long gone.

Do I fear someone jumping out at me, scaring me, harming me?

Do I fear the unknown of what is to come?

Or is what I really fear my inability to handle the future?

What harm can come to me, what is unknown to me?

I have known foolishness, failure, despair, rejection, pain, and sorrow.

What other fears are left?

I shine the light around the room, acknowledging no harm is there.

On the floor are shoes that haven't been put away.

On the counter are dishes that need to be cleaned.

On the shelves are books I don't read, photos I don't look at,
now covered in dust.

On the ceiling are cobwebs not seen since I rarely look up.

The light highlights my chores and responsibilities.

Maybe that is why the light was off, to hide these from my view.

I sit down and shut off the flashlight, plunging the room back into darkness.

As I sit there, I think about those photos of people I love, places I enjoyed.

I begin to relive them in my mind, smiling at the happy memories.

I think about the books I've kept and how the stories transported me
or taught me.

I think about the dishes on the counter, left over from a small party with
a few friends.

We laughed and talked for several hours.

I think about the shoes that got left to dry because I got caught in a rainstorm while walking.

I remember the storm, the sound of the drops hitting the various surfaces, the feel of the water running down my face, as I turned my head up. I hear the immense quite when the rain stopped and smell the clean. I feel the heat of the sun as it reappeared.

I realize my chores, my responsibilities are just the final chapter in those happy memories.

I think about my life.

I have known success, friendship, joy, and love.

I realize the flashlight in my hand wasn't what I needed to quiet my fears, I needed the flashlight inside me.

This Poem Is Not For You by Elissa Beaudoin

dear Time,

for you

I no more fear

because of him.

because of him

I know more fear

for you,

dear Time.

Water Wanders by Genevieve Weston

A boat
  Drifts
  Wanders
   I Paddle
   Slowly
    Pulling against the flow of water
     Without aim
      Weeds pulling my paddle
      Down
       Down
        Down into the water

I pull my paddle
   Against this force
    A small battle against nature
     Quickly resolved
      I continue to wander on the water

Nature sounds surround
   Birds sing gently
    Frogs chirp calmly
     Bugs hum steadily
      Breeze rustles leaves and reed

Clouds traveling slowly across blue skies
   Fertile ground casts richness into air
    Water ripe with green life
     Water wanders

What a Messy Way of Wasting Time by J.M. King

I've been spilling my blood out onto paper and watching it,
Waiting in the hopes that it would take the shape of
Every word that's been lingering in me,
I've been trying to dry every indescribable emotion
In between these pages in the form of
Oxidizing crimson.

I've been pleading with the words to flood out of me now
So that I can make peace with the emptiness instead,
Because every living, dying, and dead part of me
Knows only the words you had left behind here,
In my bed.

I would bleed out just to get rid of them.

When on an Island by Joel Hall

No two waves are the same.
Each caresses the shore differently.
With every surge forward,
Something new is brought back.

You told me your name and I asked you to repeat it.
"Marloes," you said to the rhythm of the warm water crashing at our bare feet.
Your eyes grew more green with each step we took deeper into the sea.
And in that moment, I knew I wanted to know more.

The perfumed scent you left on my hands was a bittersweet gift.
You didn't know you gave it to me before you departed for your next flight.
It lingered for hours and conjured up a phantom of you with every whiff,
Until the ocean had its chance to strip it off my hands and swallow it.

I slept in a car at the beach where we first touched.
I woke up sick and tired with the absence of your energy.
I swam in the waters you told me were too dangerous,
But you weren't there to reason with me now.

A wave lifted me up and I landed on my head.
My back folded and I washed up near the spot we sunbathed.
"I take risks, but highly calculated ones," you said to me.
"I do too, but I'm terrible at math." I replied through a grin.

I cannot navigate these waters alone.
Luckily, there is a new current in the sea, only known to you and me.
It's one that grows stronger with every word we share.
And one day, it will carry us to an island of our own making.

Blood vs Love by Gabrielle Jones

Words loose,
Searing my mind
What kind of message
Will my words leave behind?

A letter?
A poem?
A threat?
Why do I fret?

I want my words
To enlighten his mind,
With a sprinkle of compassion,
In a sea of unkind

Oh, why do I bother?
Why even doubt?
My Inspiration
Comes from, without

I have a voice,

An allie in my head,
A soft, heavy hand
That guides me instead,
Closer to Peace

My instinct,
Was to kill

To ceaselessly butcher
Like a high-powered drill

To open the door
He's banging with ham-fists,
Instinct, a challenge to ignore

To bash him in the face
With this metal stool I clutch,
'Holy hell!
When did I pick this up?'

Adrenaline surges through my viens
As I picture his bloodied brains
Strewn about the walls
Of this sullen stairwell

My plan is to smash him
Hard in the face
Gravity will carry him
All the way to the base
Of this narrow staircase

I won't be done there
My anger, too great
I'd run down those stairs,
To seal his fate

Perhaps I'd flip the switch
At the top of the stairs, first,

To have optimal viewing
Of my product of bloodthirst

I'd follow the body,
Still clutching the stool,
And bash, and bash, and bash
Until forming a decent pool,
Of dead, alcoholic blood

But even that,

Doesn't seem like enough
I will follow him to the grave!
To the depths
Harsh and rough

I'll follow him there
And show him REAL Carnage!
The Devil will just have to share,
Because,
I'm. Not. Done.

My hand crept towards the knob,
Led by Instinct,
And Bloodthirst,
And Hate
In my head,
I had already sealed our fate
But that hand
Soft, but heavy, like lead,

Rests on my arm
The deep, calm voice, says,

"Daughter, I love you,
I know how you feel
But, unlock that door,
And the pain will be real
Your future is ahead of you,
Bright as the moon,
And your brother's in blue,
Will be there soon
So slow down, breathe deep,
This is a safe zone
We'll do this together,
You're never alone"

I let go of the knob
As the footsteps retreat,
The darkness in my soul,
Accepting defeat.

It wouldn't have worked,
If not for the voice of my Father,
And that in itself,
Is why I bother
Trying to be better

It's why I try,
To walk a straight line
Not everyone is fortunate
To have a Guardian like mine

Dirty Laundry by Janellis Quintana

I had this white tee
For about 2 months
I question whether it should be kept
Or tossed

Never ending laundry
Each stain
Is only a reflection of me

If aging's a disease
And love leads to disaster
It only means what goes around
Will get back to you

If you dare to smile
You must long to cry
The way of the world is
To not hide

The rhyme is subtle
Though it took me years to realize it myself

There will come a moment where you'll leave it all behind
Skies will diminish as you become one
You won't be able to feel below
As once before

Then there it is the white shirt
In all it's stains

Memory to be kept
Idea to be cherished
All noted on that white tee

Embrace it then
Or embrace it now

The stain of your first moments
The stains of your very last
All apart of what made you

Dare to toss it
Shall it set you free?

Admire it daily
Your imperfections

I appreciate you
My favorite white tee
You will be washed

But my stains
Will remain forever

Guidance by Anthony Snider

Free us from yourself
                    - Meister Eckhart
God is in the furnace.
It's long slow breathing
confirming my conjectures.

God is of the walls. The popping
plaster's shrugs and sighs,
every tick an ordained answer
to every minuscule conundrum.
                    God is in

what is in the glass and out the window
of the sky, and yes,
in and out of my mind,
this present and attentive cosmos –
one huge omniscient theophany.

I am never alone.

I must always entertain always
mind my p's and q's
like a child in fear of holy retribution
a permanent casting out
somewhere beyond the wilderness.

I am always rehearsing
for conversations I will never have.
Thinking of Him too much can kill a man.

Kontrol All Thee Elite by Ato Dankwa

For-the "shepherd" to-"watch" the "sheep"
For-the security to-"ensure" the "fleet"
For-the "tasks" stuck on re-peat
CONTROL, ALT, DELETE!...
For those on loop in-the heap
For those bogged down in-the deep
For those on-ah dee cline steep
Hit: CONTROL, ALT, DELETE!

Ask by Jessica Wendi Abel

Each day for thirty-five years
you and your brother asked.
Often they were simple asks.
Where are my chicken nuggets?
Why is it taking so long for the movie to play?
Your asks got more complicated
during Passover, one year, when you questioned
whether or not Daddy and I
could get passed over
when we were dead in our graves.

I never want you or your brother
to feel guilty
for everything
you asked of us
the way my parents did to me.

But remember all the times
you asked to be picked up
even before you learned to talk?
Your arms outstretched while we burned the dinner
tripping over toys you threw into the kitchen?

Please don't feel as if you inconvenienced us
when we drove to the pharmacy to pick up drugs
all those evenings we intended to clean the house
when you asked for relief from the airborne illnesses
you brought home to us.

Or those Friday and Saturday nights we chose to stay home
with you and your brother instead of asking for one night with friends.
I want you to keep all this in mind when we ask
Why is it taking so long for you to give us grandchildren?
Because payback is a bitch.

Mayday by Githara Gunawardena

When did it stop being
Just portholes and sea-spray?
Cabin birthdays and your Egyptian crew-mates
And I was the prettiest little thing any of you had ever seen.

Was it when I grew taller
Than the noodle tower?
Do you remember?
We would stack those plastic boxes of ramen
From under the bunk
While amma made baby formula for me
In the cabin.
I assume those were some sort of last resort ration,
Meant for a weary sailor, hungry during a nautical mishap but
There we were, laughing
Among the confetti-remains of shattered noodle
And time you borrowed, away from the helm-
I like to think you were giving the ship up to Caribbean winds
Just to watch me laugh.

Remember coming home to us after months spent
Hardening your stomach, your heart aching?
I used to think returning

To my fat arms around your knees
And amma's kiss on your cheek
Were the happiest of those years, to you
But time has taught me that a beer belly and smoker's chest
Are the vestiges of a life that you would never leave in the contrails,
Not even for us.

Maybe you've noticed I'm sixty pounds thinner now
Than I was when you were not here for my sixteenth.
Maybe you just don't know what to say
When I voyage out into the deep end every once in a while,
Get a new tattoo,
Build a stomach to rival yours and chain-smoke while you watch
Please hear me when I whisper,
Shamefacedly
For we captains try never to blow the foghorn:

I just want to find new building blocks for our towers,
And the old porthole
To let the sun through again.